A Voice

The Mystery Finished!

The Negro has a Soul - His normal relation is that of a servant of tribute to Shem

and Japheth.

A Voice

The Mystery Finished!
The Negro has a Soul - His normal relation is that of a servant of tribute to Shem and Japheth.

ISBN/EAN: 9783337262259

Printed in Europe, USA, Canada, Australia, Japan

Cover: Foto ©Andreas Hilbeck / pixelio.de

More available books at **www.hansebooks.com**

THE MYSTERY FINISHED

THE NEGRO HAS A SOUL.

HIS NORMAL RELATION IS THAT OF A SERVANT OF TRIBUTE TO SHEM AND JAPHETH. THE NEGRO IS NOT A CITIZEN OF THE STATE, BUT A MEMBER OF THE CHURCH BY DIVINE APPOINTMENT. THE NEGRO IS ONLY MADE A CITIZEN WHILE THE "TWO WITNESSES ARE DEAD"— THESE ARE MOSES AND CHRIST, CIVIL LAW AND ECCLESIASTIC OR SOCIAL LAW. THIS DEATH IS FOR FORTY-TWO MONTHS, OR FOR THREE AND HALF YEARS.

" The sun is in the Heavens and yet a horror of great darkness covers the world."
" Shall he that contendeth with the Almighty instruct him? He that reproveth God, let him answer it,"—JOB XL:v2 XL:2.

Copyright secured according to law.

MEMPHIS:
PUBLIC LEDGER BOOK AND JOB PRINTING ESTABLISHMENT.
1868.

ERRATA.

It is due the publishers of this little work to state that its typography is more accurate than could have been reasonably expected, since the distance that separated the author and publisher made it necessary to use the mail as the only means of communication between the parties for a correct proof. The general sense at which the author has aimed has been kept throughout the whole. There are a few grammatical errors which the readers can easily correct.

The author would have preferred a more liberal use of large caps in beginning important words, and in making quotations, yet this was not expedient, and does not effect the sense. In the use of proper names, and in making quotations a few mistakes occur that mars the sense, and the most important of these deserve to be pointed out.

Page 20, 10th line, bottom, *Isaac* should be *Ishmael*. Page 24, 26th line, top, *David* should be *Daniel*. Page 33, 23d line, top, *Cainain* should be *Canaan*; same page, 25th line, *Cainian* should be *Canaan*. Page 35, 10th line, top, *our* proselyte should be *one* proselyte. Page 40, 15th line, bottom, 556 *by* 1744 should be *added to* 1744. Page 41, 10th line, top, *Ex* should be *Er*. Page 44, 13th line, top, *Othdal* should be *Othneal*. *Ehu* should be *Ehud*. Same page, 20th line, bottom, *Decemvere's* should be *Decemviri's ; Triumvini's* should be *Triumvire's*. Page 55, 3d line, top, *then* should be *there*. Page 59, 9th line, top, *divine* should be *divide*. Page 58. 20th line, bottom, *Isaac* should be *Israel*. Page 63, 11th line, bottom, *willingly* should be *wittingly*. Page 66, 10th line, bottom, "Thou shalt *not* suffer," should read, "Thou shalt suffer." Page 77, 13th line, top, Joshua *Saul*, should be Joshua *Soule*. Page 96, 18th line, top, *creatures* should be *creations ;* same line, *they* should be *there*. Page 107, 13th line, bottom, *there* should be *thine*. Page 123. 8th line, bottom, leave out *the tribe of*. Page 126, 19th line, bottom, *Judah* should read *Judas*.

The author would take this occasion to speak to that small class of minds who take an interest in the recondite questions contained in this little work. The greater dilligence employed in attempting to comprehend the subject, the better will you be prepared to appreciate a more elaborate presentation of the same, when the proper time arrives—that time is not yet. Would you learn, you must study with great care. This book may be had of the book-sellers of Memphis. Price, $1.

THE AUTHOR.

THE MYSTERY FINISHED!

THE NEGRO HAS A SOUL.

HIS NORMAL RELATION IS THAT OF A SERVANT OF TRIBUTE TO SHEM AND JAPHETH. THE NEGRO IS NOT A CITIZEN OF THE STATE, BUT A MEMBER OF THE CHURCH BY DIVINE AP-MENT. THE NEGRO IS ONLY MADE A CITIZEN WHILE THE "TWO WITNESSES ARE DEAD"— THESE ARE MOSES AND CHRIST, CIVIL LAW AND ECCLESIASTIC OR SOCIAL LAW. THIS DEATH IS FOR FOR-TY-TWO MONTHS, OR FOR THREE AND HALF YEARS.

" The sun is in the Heavens and yet a horror of great darkness covers the world."
" Shall he that contendeth with the Almighty instruct him? He that reproveth God, let him answer it."—JOB XL:v2 XL:2.

MEMPHIS:
PUBLIC LEDGER BOOK AND JOB PRINTING ESTABLISHMENT.
1868.

PREFACE.

This little work is presented to the public as the synopsis of a larger work, written by the author during this great civil war in the Japhetic Israel.

It is based upon God's symbols; keeping up the transfers from one to another, from Adam down to the tribes, or States, of this South land.

The entire history of Israel was given by God to Moses in the Mount. The three patriarchs, Abraham, Isaac and Jacob, move as the Trinity in the Godhead. The wives of these move with the Church, or soul, as Israel has moved. The twelve tribes are representatives of human laws, as they would mix the "Nchash," or "Nackhash," with the laws of God.

The tribes of this South land are given to draw the distinction between the laws of God and the laws of Nature, or the "Nahash;" and they finish The Mystery.

No nation, no prince, can legislate wisely, that does not understand the difference between these, as God demonstrates them himself.

The reader must study in order to learn the symbolic meaning of names and things, and how to keep up the transfer of one to the other. In this outline, the author has avoided speculation, and deals only with facts.

None need inquire who the author is. His history is so obscure that he would hardly be suspected by his neighbors of appearing before the public as an author, to enlighten that public. He has never preached a sermon, and never filled any public station in civil life, and never was a lecturer on any subject, and never went anywhere, and never saw the capital of a single State in this land. These thoughts are fully dedicated to all writers on prophecy.

THE AUTHOR.

THE MYSTERY FINISHED.

"For it is written: Abraham had two sons: the one by a bondmaid, the other by a free-woman."

"But he who was of the bond woman was born after the flesh: but he of the free-woman was by promise. Which things are an allegory, for these are the two covenants."—Gal. iv. 22d and 24th.

God has given the world one Book, and has also given the world a history as the exponent of the sense of that Book.

If this Book tells to man that he has two natures, the one as natural, and the other as supernatural, it also tells him that both these natures shall be brought under the reign of the laws of the Creator, which are given for the government of both the natural and the supernatural man. This Book teaches not only how man will act in following the laws of his nature, as the natural, in both departments of that nature; but also how God, the Creator, will act in over-ruling that nature, and subjecting it to his own laws. It tells the times when, the manner how, and the place where, this will be done.

If this Book talks of two cherubims seated upon either end of the seat of mercy, it is itself the two cherubims. Moses and twelve patriarchs make one cherubim; Christ and twelve apostles make the other. If these are looking into the veiled ark, over which the wings of the cherubim meet, so is the Book veiled in the middle by four great prophets and twelve minor ones.

Four books of law and twelve patriarchs make the body; four books of gospel, with twelve apostles, make the soul to the body.

These two will unite upon the truths taught by four great prophets and twelve less ones, and then will "the world become a living soul," and the angel will fly, "having the everlasting gospel to preach."

These two cherubims are called by various names in

the Book. They are the "two witnesses." They are the "two anointed ones." They are the "two olive branches." Peace to the world dwells alone between these olive branches. They are Sinai and Jerusalem. They are God's two spies, Joshua and Caleb, sent out to watch a wicked world, that follows the laws of the beast, or laws of nature, and not the laws of God.

These two spies have made a good report, and say, "they are fully able to take the world," and they will do it, regardless of any different report made by other parties concerning Anek, or Amelek, or Og, or all other giants in the land.

These witnesses, as the laws of God for his creature man, will add the "plagues of the Book to the world, until men cease to mend it, and take it as it is." These hold the sword, and will guard the way to the "tree of knowledge," which, when man reaches, it will be found to be simple obedience to the laws of the Creator, without the smallest amendment from the laws of nature.

No other ark than this can ride a world safely over the waste of waters, and bring it into port. This ark has a lower, and an upper, and a middle story, and it is pitched within and without. It looks to both the outer and the inner man, in his civil and soul laws. These witnesses of God, like their heads, Moses and Christ, refuse to be made a king, according to the laws of the natural man. Pharaoh's daughter will plead in vain for Moses. The Israel of law, from Japheth, like that of law from Shem, may try by force to elevate the law of Christ, standing for "the Christ," to the supreme power, it will be of no use. God will fill his own types by his own laws.

Various names, or things, are used to represent these laws, or witnesses, of God. They are called moon and sun. They are called husband and bride. They are called Jerusalem. They are called Abraham and Melkezedek. They are called body and soul. They are called law and gospel, civil and Church. The book that teaches them is called Rachel. As the literal Rachel stole the literal gods of Laban, so the Book Rachel will steal all the gods out of the world. If the two witnesses be named, the one is Benjamin, the other is Joseph. If the literal Benjamin has ten literal sons to represent law, these are the ten commandments of the law of Moses for the bodily man. If the literal Joseph has two sons, as Ephraim and Manassah, these are law and gospel. These are the children over which Rachel weeps, and she never can be comforted while these are not.

As sure as Joseph was made head of the "red-headed

dragon " of Egypt, and brought all his brethren to him, so sure will the laws of God, for which Joseph stands, bring all the kings and kingdoms of the world, for which his brethren stand, to the laws of Christ, upon whom they met.

Let the dragon of Egypt pursue. Let the beast of Babylon carry into captivity. Let "the false prophets" cry "crucify him." God will give us a king to serve us according to our liking. Let the archers shoot at Joseph, standing for the laws of God. " His bow will abide in strength, being upheld by the mighty God of Jacob."

These laws of God met in Moses, born of Levi, as civil and ceremonial. They met on David, the seventh son of Jesse, the type of Christ, born of the tribe of Judah, as civil and gospel law. They met on the Christ, born of the tribe of Judah, as civil and gospel, and he fulfilled the whole law, as set in David, as a union of the two in one ; but not as subjecting the world to his reign, as David took possession of all the land promised him in Canaan, as the type of the world to be subjected to the reign of " the Christ." This remains yet to be done.

God has two sons to represent his laws. These are Christ and Moses; Joseph and Benjamin.

Christ is before Moses : yet the law of Moses for the body, is before the law of Christ for the soul. Benjamin is before Joseph, in whom the double laws meet. The same is true in reference to Shem and Japheth. Japheth, to whom gospel is given, is older than Shem, to whom law was given. As in the elder, the double laws are to meet, the younger, in either case, standing alone, as civil law precedes the elder. The first born, in either case, is by the deeds of the law, and is of the bond-woman. The last born is by promise, and is the first begotten, though not the first born.

God said to Moses : "Say ye to Pharaoh, Israel is my son, even my first born ; let my son go, that he may serve me." This first born son was Moses and twelve patriarchs, the literal sons of the literal Jacob. The first begotten son is Christ, with twelve apostles. The first born is the literal man, made of the dust. The first begotten is the breathing of God into this dust. These two shall become one, as man, made of two natures, is one. That the law of God, as given by Moses for the civil man, and the gospel, as given by Christ, for the soul of man, shall unite in a literal nation, literally descended from Japheth, is the decree of God. These laws make the kingdom of God in contrast with the kingdom of men.

The watchmen shall come to see eye to eye. "There shall be one shepherd and one fold." The two literal tribes, between which Jerusalem was built, as Benjamin and Judah, are law and gospel. The Christ came between Benjamin, as law, and Judah, as gospel.

The laws that met in the literal Jerusalem, met on him, and he became the substitute of the literal house. "Destroy this temple, and I will build it in three days." These laws are that Jerusalem that is to "become the praise of the whole earth."

The laws of God, as his two witnesses, given to the Israel from Shem, not only taught the laws by the use of words, but every act in both had a symbolic meaning, which stands as a prophetic sign, to be repeated in gospel, Israel given to Japheth.

These laws stand to each other as type and anti-type, each of which had to be repeated in the land in which Japheth was to be "enlarged over Shem." America is the land in which Japheth is enlarged over Shem. When Noah said: "Blessed is Shem, and Canaan shall be his servant," direct reference was had to the literal Israel, the descendants of Jacob, as God's types to whom the laws and the prophets were to be given. Canaan, the son of Ham, was also the type of the servant of tribute, when Noah said: "God will enlarge Japheth; he shall dwell in the tents of Shem, and Canaan shall be his servant."

Direct reference was had to the land of America, which Shem first held in the person of Red Esau, the brother of Jacob. This Esau, or Shem, was a man of the "quiver and the bow." He hunted venison. He scorned his birthright. He lived in tents. When it is said: "Canaan shall be his servant," respect is had to literal Canaan as the type, and also the law of Moses, as given in the land of Canaan. The two covenants set in Abraham, were predicated upon the two prophecies of Noah. The first was of the bond-woman, or was bound by the law of the literal man.

The second was of the free-woman, and would be, by choice, under the Divine guidance. The first covenant was with Abram, which had Canaan, the son of Ham, for the servant of tribute. The second was with Abra-Ham, which changed the son Canaan to Ham, the father of Canaan.

The law which changed Abram to Abraham, is a law of faith in God and his word, both in reference to the civil and soul law. It is the admission that the Creator knows what is best for the creature, without respect to the laws of the beast or nature. If the one says: "Thou shalt have no gods before me," the other says: "Ye must be born again." If the one says: "Thou shalt not kill, nor steal, nor covet thy neighbor's servant," the other says: "Blessed are the peacemakers:" "Blessed are the meek:" "Servants, be obedient to your masters." The laws of the natural man rise up in opposition to these laws of God, and say: "Force is king; thou shalt kill; thou shalt steal; to the victors belong the spoils; all men are equal," etc. The natural law of the soul says: "Do religion: the fruits of the body may atone for the sin of the soul. It asks, in reference to the law of God: "How can these things be?" Between these two thieves, as natural laws, the Christ is crucified. The law of God is the word of God. Whether these laws are made flesh, in the person of "the Christ," or in a nation of "the Christ," they will be spoken of as one and the same. The coming of the laws is the coming of Christ.

As the Israel of law, from Shem, made up of twelve patriarchs and Moses, as the law-giver killed the second son, as Christ and twelve apostles, so have the twelve tribes of law, in this land of Japheth, killed the twelve of both law and gospel. Both say: "By our law he ought to die." The work at which we are aiming, is to set forth, by this latter Israel, what is that symbolic sense, as principles of human laws, that God attached to the twelve tribes of Israel. No king, nor emperor, nor republic, can legislate wisely without a knowledge of these facts.

With the twelve tribes in Shem, God sealed the Book. With the twelve tribes in Japheth, he has "unsealed it," and "finished his mystery."

There has never been one mistake nor one accident, down that line of Israel which God selected to prove to his creature man, his right to rule him. The entire history of literal Israel was a type of something to follow after. The prophets tell of things to come, in the history of Israel. It follows, from hence, that every prophecy has its predicate upon the literal acts of the literal Israel.

The acts of both the Israels, from Shem as the type, and that of Japhet as the anti type, were each acted out by the literal parties, as recorded in the book of Genesis. This book was given by God to Moses in the Mount. It is a prophecy, in action, of the entire history of Israel, from the first Adam to the crowning of the second Adam "Lord of the world." There is not one word of tradition in the book. It is too contradictory to be traditional. It is too exact in its application to Israel's history not to be prophetic.

All the prophets speak of things future, as having already passed, or as passing at the time in which they are mentioned. The same facts apply to the books of Genesis and Job. These belong to the entire history of Israel, without respect to the literal account assumed as a basis upon which the prophecies are founded. The things written by Moses in these books, were written to be understood in the latter days of the Japhetic Israel. There is not one mistake in all of God's book. There is nothing wanting, and nothing too much. Babylon has confused the world long enough; man must come to Jerusalem to learn.

When God said to Moses: "See thou make all things after the pattern showed thee in the Mount," it was because that that was made was good.

It would be about as easy to find a mistake in the physical world, or in the celestial heavens, as to find one in God's book. These, together with the moral world, are all formed in one mould, and the one is given to explain the other.

The question to be presented is one of vast proportions, and the slightest glance at the most prominent points is all that can be indulged in this running outline. The laws of God are made separate and distinct from the laws of man, by those typical characters which God used as the representatives of laws. Man is a trinity. The God-head is a trinity. Israel is a trinity. God works with a trinity; first, the two halves, and then the whole. In order to reach the truth, the distinct ideas attached to the trinities of God, must be understood. Cain, Abel, Seth, are ideas to be applied to Israel's history. The same is true in reference to Shem, Ham, Japheth; or Abraham, Isaac, Jacob; or Saul, David, Solomon; or Noah, Daniel, Job; or Father, Son, and Holy Ghost; or Law, Gospel and Millennial Kingdoms. These are called Kingdom, Power, Glory. These are trinities, because of the distinct ideas they are given to illustrate, either as laws of God, or of the natural man.

Three times does Balaam, the prophet of Baal, or the natural man, move his locality, to curse Israel. There are three invitations to the great supper. It is at the last that men are compelled to come in. This is because God finishes his demonstration to man, that he will rule him by his own laws. Three times is Christ tempted. Three go in the furnace, etc. This idea is carried out in the natural world. The moon, the sun, the earth. As the sun and moon give value to the earth, so will law and gospel make this earth as the New Jerusalem. Asia, Africa, Europe, are but a different form of presenting Shem, Ham, Japheth. The two united, as Asia and Europe, are Shem and Japheth, or law and gospel. These are the two to put the garment upon their shoulders, and walk backward, and cover the nakedness of a drunken world.

As the Christ came in between these, in the center of

the Eastern world, and upon whom the laws of God met, so has the nation of "the Christ" to bring forth "the fruits of the kingdom," met in the center of the Western world, between Shem and Japheth; and Japheth has taken possession of Shem, not only in literal fact, but also in the laws for both body and soul, civil and church, which Shem rejected; and hence Japheth is, in a double sense, "enlarged over Shem."

This enlargement is first with an Israel of law, standing for twelve patriarchs, or the body, or civil law of the body; and secondly, with a nation, not only answering to the twelve as law, but also answering to the twelve apostles as gospel, or as adding the soul to the body. These latter twelve will tell the world what is both law and gospel.

The genealogy is perfect when the diverging lines meet and agree in one. Let this idea be clearly understood. Cain is the literal, or bodily, man, and God's law of the body. God requires he should offer the fruits of the ground. The genealogy of Cain sets the world's civil or political governments down the line of Israel, closing with Lamech. Abel is "the Christ," or soul, of the world, and his faith is the law of God, in reference to "the Christ." Seth, who came in the stead of Abel, stands to represent the soul, or church of the soul, and his line closes with Lamech, the father of Noah. When these two lines meet, in literal fact, according to the symbols of each, then is the genealogy perfect, and the laws in which they meet will make the ark to save the world. While the two lines of Cain and Seth are given to represent the soul and body of man, or civil and church laws, the two lines from Shem and Japheth are both political in reference to their genealogy. The line of Shem is the same in number with that of Seth, and closes with Meshech. The line of Japheth is the same in number with that of Cain, and has Tiras following his Meshech. There is no accident in this arrangement, nor in anything else written in God's Book.

The land of Meshech, from Shem, was the most eastern part of his land, as Asia, which was, doubtless, once North America. The land of Meshech, from Japheth, was the western part of his land, as Europe. These two, as Meshech from Shem, and Meshech from Japheth, have met in this land, and the Meshech from Japheth has driven out the Meshech from Shem, and he is enlarged over him. As these facts are literally fulfilled, so the literal facts concerning the Lamech from Cain, as the civil law, and the Lamech from Seth, as the church law, will be seen to be one, as Adam and Eve were one. Truely does Eli-as," the God-servant, "restore all things."

"I am the first and the last," means that those symbols with which God started, are the same with which he closes. He changes not. The Bible is as round as the world. The Old and New Testaments are one. They are body and soul. Not a change between Moses and Christ, but David, the king of the gospel dispensation, made it before Christ came. Moses and David were the civil laws of the same people. David changed the ceremonial to gospel. David never offered a literal sacrifice, such as Moses used. His sacrifices are of the heart—the inner, and not the outer man. David, as civil and soul laws, is the same as Joseph, or as the three patriarchs, Abraham, Isaac and Jacob. It was not David that killed Goliah, representing all heathen political governments. It was God, using David as his type. It was not David that put Uriah in the front of the battle. It was God, using David as his prophet, to show how he would kill all human governments for the Church, that he might get Bathsheba to bring forth Solomon, the eighth, and last, and highest type of Christ. It was not David that had seven wives and ten concubines. It was God representing himself by seven churches, and ten nations out of which they were to come. It was not the literal Solomon that had three hundred concubines and seven hundred wives. It was God representing his own actions by Solomon, and showing how he would take all the political nations and all the churches out of the world. Nothing is by accident. It is not Abraham, but "God the Father," that has Hagar and Ishmael to represent the ceremonial law, and Sarah and Isaac to stand for gospel. It is Isaac, as God the Son, that has one wife, Rebecca, and whose volition is consulted about becoming a wife. Rebecca is the gospel church, in contrast with Hagar and Sarah, as laws of the church. It is Jacob, as God the Holy Ghost, combining Father and Son, that has two wives—Leah and Rachel—and their two maid-servants for wives, to set forth the principles of the Divine Government. Until one single church is found to agree with a civil government, and both are the seventh, to agree with David, the seventh son, or with Joseph, the seventh type of Christ; with the lawgivers of both, out of Judah; or "from between his feet," in the Japhetic Israel, the same as the type set in Shem, together with a score of other positive facts, it will be in vain to look for the husband and the bride, according to God's prophetic truth.

Following God's facts and God's fulfilment are the only guides to lead to this result.

The characters of the New Testament are to those of the Old as the literal seed of Jacob are to the spiritual Jacob, as

"God the Holy Ghost." If the one is born by natural laws, the other is begotten by the Holy Ghost, and yet all the natural laws are observed in those thus begotton. They are not only soul, but they are body and soul. The twelve apostles are to the twelve patriarchs as soul to body. If the twelve in one case are represented by one sister, as Dinah standing for the church, or soul of the whole, so the twelve in the other are represented by one, as Paul standing as the summary of the whole. If a king, as Saul of Benjamin, stands to represent the first—saying God had no right to transfer the government to Judah or David—he finds his representative, as "Saul of Tarsus," persecuting unto death.

If there were fifteen patriarchs, the regular twelve, the two of Joseph, and the daughter Dinah standing as the sun amid these signs of the zodiac, the same is true in reference to the apostles. These are the twelve and the two set for apostles, Justus and Mathias, and Paul standing for the whole, as to him was committed the care of all the churches.

If the tribe Levi stood for the church among the tribes, so when it is transferred to Judah, as gospel, the first evangelist, as Matthew is named Levi, to show how the transfer was made. To Joseph among the patriarchs the birthright was given, and upon him God's laws unite. So the Joseph the son of Jacob of the New Testament is the reputed father of Christ, upon whom the laws of God met. The Mary, the literal mother of the Christ, is the representative of the embodied church, to bring forth the nation of " the Christ," which is to take the laws of God. It is not only through Mary, as the harlot Rahab, or Naamah, or Naomi, but also through Elizabeth, as Ruth, or England, who stands for the mother of John, the forerunner, but it will be through Andrew, as the first apostle in this land, born of the tribe of Judah. There is no need to run in advance of God's types in Shem, and their fulfillment in Japheth.

The Simeon of the New Testament is the Simeon of the Old. The tribe of Simeon, the second son of Jacob, is the literal tribe to represent force in civil government. If Reuben, the first son, stands for the first Israel from Shem, as in Palestine. Simeon, the second, will stand for the second or forcible Israel, in Japheth, as in Rome. If Reuben, the first, stands for the first colony of this land, as Virginia, Simeon, the second, will stand for the second, as the Plymouth colony. Joseph takes Simeon and binds him, in the presence of all his brethren, saying: "Bring me Benjamin, and I will release Simeon," the literal sense of which is: Bring me the law of Moses, and this forcible Simeon will leave the world. Moses, when blessing the tribes, leaves out Simeon.

Simeon, as force having been used as God's whip of cords, to drive Israel to demonstrate the meaning of God's dual laws for man, is no longer needed. When Simeon, as force has done this, as these laws will stand to the world as the Christ, upon whom they meet—this Simeon will say: "Now, Lord, lettest thou thy servant depart in peace, for mine eyes have seen thy salvation." That salvation is Moses, for the civil man, and Christ, for the church, or soul of man.

The tribes of the literal Israel divide at the tribe of Gad, which is the seventh, and is the tribe to set the second half of this Japhetic Israel. The doubting Thomas is the apostle to set the division between the twelve apostles. Use will be had for every fact in this Japhetic Israel given to "Unseal the Book."

As Moses was a sign to the literal Israel, so Christ is a sign to the Japhetic, or gospel Israel. "This child is set for the fall and rising again of many in Israel, and for a sign which shall be spoken against."

The literal acts of the literal Christ were symbols of things to follow after. As he was crucified between two thieves, so are his laws crucified between the double laws of man's nature. If not a bone of him was broken, the meaning is, not a law of his shall fail.

If he casts seven devils out of Mary Magdalene, it has the same meaning as the seven washings of Naaman in Jordan; or the seven times that passed over Nebuchadnezzar, who ate grass like an ox, or followed the law of the beast. It is the seven efforts of God to cleanse the moral world; the same as the seven strata to form the geological or physical world. If Christ says to Mary: "Touch me not, Mary; I have not yet ascended to my Father and your Father," it is the prophetic sign given, that when God's two witnesses meet in a nation of Japheth, they would be "caught up to God and his throne" three years and a-half, and then return again. There is nothing to show any verity of fact in reference to the literal act. If Christ is three times anointed, it is to fill the three anointings of David, both of which will find their anti-type in the Japhetic Israel of both law and gospel. If Pilate says: "What I have written, I have written," it is the prophetic sign that Christ will make the name of reproach good, and it shall not be altered; as if he had said: I am the king of this world, and mean to govern it by my own laws; and though these laws, like their master, prophecy in sackcloth and ashes, I will, with all their reproach, conquer the world to their dominion.

Whatever rises to power, either as civil or church laws, before my measured times of reproach, are laws of men, and not my laws. In the fullness of time I will show this world who and what they are.

While the apostle Andrew is the first apostle brought to Christ by John, the fore-runner, ("Andrew first findeth his brother, Simon Peter,") it is the three apostles, James, Peter, John, that are used as the trinity of apostles, to represent law, gospel and millennial kingdoms. James is law; Peter is the apostle whose literal actions are prophetic signs of the gospel Israel. He moves as the gospel Israel has moved. The law of flesh and blood did not reveal to Peter that the Christ was the son of God.

Nor is the gospel thus revealed. This typical revelation of God to the world did not convert Peter, nor did it convert the world. "The man of sin" had to come in, and sit in the temple of God, and claim to legislate for both departments of God's kingdom. Like Peter, he drew the sword to defend his faith. All these prophetic signs had to be fulfilled before the expiration of Daniel's 2,300 years to "cleanse the sanctuary of the heart;" to which we will come after awhile. Rome has done right in claiming Peter as holding the keys of the gospel kingdom. She will be converted, and come to the truth, as did Peter, at the appointed time. God's truth will neither bend nor break at human opinions. The seven churches are all legitimate and proper (as will be seen in due time), in God's demonstration. They are the seven wives of David. The Bathsheba of the seven will also be pointed out. John is the millennial apostle. It is not the literal John, but the character of John, that is to remain till the last and final judgment. "If he tarry till I come," means, if that character he presents is the only one that will remain in the glorious disposation. "What is that to thee?" You must fill your separate types, as well as he. John is used in the same sense as the trinity. Noah, Daniel, Job. These are the characters that will be left when God commands the sword to go through the land. When Christ said to his mother: "Woman, behold thy son: son, behold thy mother," they were spoken of as husband and bride, as representing earthly laws and heavenly laws.

James, and his brother, John, are the same in gospel as the two sons of Rachel—Benjamin and Joseph—are, in law. They are law and gospel. Andrew, and Peter, his brother, are the same as the first and second sons of Leah, as Reuben and Simeon.

As the apostle John is the millennial apostle, so he closes the revelations of God to man. John always begins at the beginning. As the characters in Genesis set the entire history of Israel, so does John go through that entire history. If he writes as an evangelist, he begins at the beginning. "In the beginning was the word," etc. If to the Elect Lady, as the church, again he repeats: "That which ye heard from the beginning." Again, in the Revelations, he repeats: "I am the first and the last." His seven trumpets, or seven seals, or seven vials, apply to the whole history of Israel, and are the seven nations, each with seven heads, down the line of God's demonstration. If Genesis has a Benjamin and Joseph to represent the laws of God: or a Manassah and Ephraim, sons of Joseph, standing for God's laws. John has a "tree of life growing upon either bank of the river, whose leaves are for the healing of the nations."

The book of Revelations laps around upon Genesis, and the book is as round as the world.

The characters of the Old Testament are the same as those in the New, and these two are one. They were given in halves to the Israel of law as Shem, as man was made in halves; first, the body, and then the soul to the body; and each of these halves were to be repeated in the Israel of Japheth. The seven ewe lambs, which Abraham set each to themselves, in a covenant made between Abraham and Abimelech, are the symbols of the seven churches of Asia, by St. John. John to the seven churches of Asia, is John to the seven churches of the land of Shem, and also John to the seven churches of the land in which Japheth is "enlarged over Shem." Shem and Japheth "walked backwards," or brought the world back to the starting point. If Shem traveled from the center of the Eastern world eastward, Japheth traveled westward. North America is the only continent that can answer to the description of the land of Eden, in which dwelt the first Adam and Eve, as body and soul, and it is likewise the place of the union of the two by the second Adam. If John crosses the Ægean sea, to reach the lonely isle in which to lay the scene of his prophecy to the seven churches, it is a prophecy in action, the same as Jacob crossing the brook Jabbok, and then recrossing to wrestle with the angel. Each act will find its correspondent in the Japhetic Israel. Every marvellous event, every pillar of stone erected, every child born by promise, and every time the phrase, "remaning unto this day," occurs—these are notes of attention, given in the Israel of Shem, to look for their correspondents in the Israel of Japheth. The same facts apply to every change of name, such as Abram and Abraham,—Jacob and Israel,—Jethro and Reuel,—Naamah and Naomi,—Sarai and Sarah,—Cainan and Kenite, etc.

A vast multitude in these modern times seem to be looking for the re-settlement of the Israel of Shem in Palestine, and the rebuilding of the literal Jerusalem. Able writers are advocating this as the scripture doctrine. The whole of the Israel of Shem was a literal type to represent the laws of God. The last dreadful act in which they were overthrown by the Romans, when the Christians escaped, was the literal representation of the last and final judgment, when all who have taken refuge in Christ will escape the vengeance of the destroyer.

Every part of the literal Jerusalem was a symbol. The rites and ordinances; the priests and sacrifices; the inner and the outer courts; the Holy Place and the Holy of Holies. Will the next Jerusalem have all these symbols attached? Will a type repeat itself? Will it be covered with the gold of Ophir? Will the noise of a hammer be heard upon it? Will it have its lower order of priests, and its high-priests entering once a year with the blood of beasts to offer for the sins of the people? Will it be Jerusalem without all these things? God moves forward to demonstrate his own truths by his own types, and men linger behind.

The great Martin Luther could not allow the symbol in the saying of Christ: "This is my body." If Rome worships beads and necklace, and the filings from the apostles' chains, as literal things, how much better does the Protestant world act in holding that literal symbols will repeat themselves? If holy monks keep watch over the sepulchre of Christ (which has been used as a type, and which has accomplished all that was intended), as though they expected him to rise every moment, how much better does the Protestant world act in looking for the rebuilding of the literal Jerusalem? The treading down Jerusalem for forty and two months, is the treading down the laws of God, for which Jerusalem stood, for forty and two months. When these laws stand upon their feet, Jerusalem is rebuilt. These laws are Benjamin and Joseph, or Benjamin and Judah. Judah is the active tribe to bring the laws typed by Joseph. The kingdom was to be taken from Shem and given to a nation bringing forth the fruits thereof. Men will have it given back to the nation from which it was taken, in direct contradiction of the plain teaching of Christ. Shem, as Asia, had law; Japheth as Europe, had gospel.

If Shem refused gospel, Japheth never had law. These brothers have alike been stubborn and stiff-necked. Law is Moses; gospel is Christ. Shem says it is all Moses; Japheth says it is all Christ. The nation to bring the two together, was to be literally from Japheth. When the one-half, as Asia, or Shem, takes gospel, the other half, as Europe, or Japheth, will take law. Shem will ask: Do not the Scriptures positively affirm that Israel shall be settled after his old estates; that the judges shall be restored, as at the beginning, and that Jerusalem shall be rebuilt in her own place, and that David shall sit upon the throne? etc. Certainly they do.

The Israel from Japheth will ask: Do not the Scriptures positively affirm that the Godhead consists of Father, Son and Holy Ghost, and that these three are one? It so teaches. Now, if God chooses Shem in Asia, to act the part of the Father, and Japheth in Europe, to act the part of the Son, and Shem and Japheth jointly in America, to act the part of the Holy Ghost, will not the very same language be used in reference to either part of this Israel, and will it not be Israel as much in one wing as the other, or as in both combined? Israel is as essentially one Israel, though made up of different parts, as man is one man, though made up of different parts.

If every prophecy, whether uttered in words or actions, meets in this land in which Japheth is "enlarged over Shem," and Jerusalem is here rebuilt by God's own types, then does it follow that this is the Israel referred to by the the prophets, and that this is God's chosen land with which to "finish his mystery," and tell the meaning to be attached to the twelve patriarchs as civil law, and to the twelve apostles as gospel law. These laws will restore David upon the throne, and give him his three anointings, as the king, according to the literal types. Does the reader ask, can this be done? If it is not done, the fault will be with the feeble agent using God's facts, that are as weighty as a "weaver's beam," and not with the facts themselves. These truths demand all the mental powers of the greatest giant. They have hitherto baffled all the skill of the learned, whether these be theologians, philosophers, statesmen, or the would-be prophets. The reader cannot be more astonished than is the writer, that one who makes no pretensions at human learning, who is, in truth, the veriest stripling in human knowledge, in God's Creation, should attempt to pilot the ship when so many great ones have foundered. We are impelled forward by the light of God's truth, and the force of his demonstration, and wonder with amazement at that horror of darkness that covers the world, with the noon-day sun in the heavens.

The account given in the book of Genesis of the antideluvian world, is the history of the post-deluvian world. It is a prophecy in action, but not in words.

What is the sense of a prophetic action? If Isaiah goes naked and barefoot, it is the sign that Israel, to whom he belongs, and of which he writes, will go naked and barefoot. If Jeremiah writes a prophecy concerning Babylon, and has it read, and orders it to be tied to a stone and cast into the Euphrates, it is a prophetic sign of the fate of Babylon. If Ezekiel is bound to his couch, upon one side, three hundred and ninety days, and then turned upon the other forty days, with a command not to turn from side to side, and with his pan and tile of brick erects his fortification and goes through the siege of Jerusalem, it is a prophecy in action. If Ahijah meets Jeroboam and tears his new garment into two parts, and one piece into ten, it is a prophecy concerning the division of Israel. If Paul is bound with the girdle of Agebus, it is a prophecy in action. If the apostles are commanded to shake the dust from their feet against an unworthy city, it is a prophecy in action. If Moses lifts the brazen serpent, it is a prophetic sign, and a prophecy in action. These examples are so numerous, it may be said that not only all the prophets, but the whole Book is a prophecy in action. God uniformly has a synopsis and a summary. Both the synopsis and the summary cover the whole ground. If Genesis is the synopsis, Revelations is the summary. A few chapters at the first of Job is the synopsis. The settlement of Job, with the same number of sons and daughters as at the start, is the summary. The seven first verses of that noted prophecy of Ezekiel in his xxxviii and xxxix, chapters, concerning a great civil war in the Japhetic Israel (and in reference to which no historian will ever write so good a history as God's prophet wrote 2500 years ago), is the synopsis; the close with Israel triumphant, and the Spirit of God poured upon him, is the summary. If Joshua compasses Jericho one time, and is ordered to go round it thus seven times in seven days, and on the last day goes round it seven times, as much is done on the last day as during the whole seven; it is the summary of the whole. The same facts apply to the measures of time. The jubilee at the end of seven times seven years, was the summary of the whole, and completed the cycle. The same truth applies to those characters used in the summaries of laws.

David and Joseph are twice counted. Jesse had but seven sons, yet David is annointed by Samuel as the eighth son of Jesse. David is first counted with the seven, and then stands for the whole constellation. Jacob went down to Egypt with sixty-six souls. The two of Joseph made sixty-eight. The account states that all the souls of Jacob were seventy souls. The sixty-eight souls, are the sixty-eight constellation of stars in the heavens, without the twelve in the zodiac. These twelve are the twelve patriarchs or the twelve apostles. Joseph is twice counted as both sun and moon, to make out the seventy, and to agree with the other seventy also appointed. In this same sense are all the kings the world has had brought together in this land, that they may be slain at once. A tribe is given to set forth these kings, and the forms of religion each has had. These, as an act of sovereignty with God, are made to act the parts for which they have stood in Israel's history. As these have hitherto acted towards God's laws, they are here made to repeat the same in reference to those laws, that they may be pointed out to men.

It has been left for this Japhetic Israel of "the last days" to tell the meaning of the battle of the world's kings, in which four killed five. The account states that Abraham pursued the four to Dan, and brought back all that had been captured. It was a prophecy in action. In literal fact, there was no such city as Dan at the time of the pursuit. The tribe of Dan, from whom the city Dan took its name, was, at the time the account was written, in the loins of Abraham. It was a prophecy of what would be in the Japhetic Israel. Instances of this sort are so numerous, it is not worth while to name them.

Reuben, the first born son of Jacob, says: "If I bring not Benjamin, slay my two sons." Literal Reuben had four sons at the time the declaration was made. The two sons of this Reuben, in this land, will be pointed out. If Hager is cast out, with her son as a little lad, and a bottle of water, and when she lays him under a shrub to die, withdraws that she may not witness the dying agony of the child, it is a prophecy in action, and the literal facts abate that sympathy which so touching a narrative kindles. What are the literal facts? Ishmael was thirteen years old when he was circumcised, at the promise of the birth of Isaac. It was not till the weaning time of Isaac that Hager and her son were cast out.

Isaac could not have been less than sixteen years old, probably several years older, when he was cast out. Both accounts are prophetic, as symbols to Israel's history. They are given in reference to the future history of Israel, and that they could not be literal acts, is the truth. All these acts hold the same relation to Israel's history that the declaration of David does, when he says: "When we were carried captive to Babylon, we hung our harps upon the willows." David never saw Babylon. This is a prophecy of a future event that will happen to those tribes that stand for the laws that met on David, spoken of as if it had already passed. These are literal acts of future things, the same in substance as all the prophecies that speak of seeing and hearing things that lay thousands of years in the distance. Let this idea be enlarged so as to get the full sense. The history of Israel is a triangle. Each side of this triangle is subject to the same laws and to the same prophecies. Each side has a dragon, a beast and a false prophet. These sides are Shem, or the Israel of law, in Judea; and Japheth, or gospel, in Europe and America, as the land in which Japheth is enlarged, in a double sense, over Shem. The dragon pursues and kills. The beast carries into captivity. The false prophet claims a higher law than Moses. Egypt was the dragon to Shem; Babylon was the beast. The literal Israel, combining with pagan Rome, were the false prophet. The higher law than Moses said, Cæsar is our king. Moses said: "Thou shalt not kill." The higher law said: "By our law he ought to die." Egypt is the place of learning. Babylon is the place of one language, and also the place of confusion.

Turning to the second side of this triangle in the land of Japheth, or gospel Israel in Rome, Pagan Rome is the dragon to kill; Papal Rome is the beast, or mystical Babylon, to lead into captivity. Mahomet stands as "the false prophet," claiming a law superior to that of Moses. If literal Babylon represents the two tribes, as Benjamin and Judah, or law and gospel, in captivity, these two are symbolically the same as the laws of God, for which David stood, and David is in captivity to literal Babylon. While two tribes are in literal Babylon, it is the other half of Israel, or the ten tribes, or the lost Ephraim, that represents "mystical Babylon." The ten kingdoms of Daniel, into which West Rome was broken, are called ten horns, and among which a "little horn" came up, and are the ten lost tribes of the Israel of Shem, given to Japheth, and they are called Ephraim. Where, among these ten, is David, that he is in captivity to mystical Babylon? This Babylon is the place of one language, the same as the literal Babylon. The Latin is the universal language.

David's harp is upon the willows. David is in the same place that Rachel is. Rachel is the woman with two wings of a great eagle hid in the place which God had prepared for her. These two wings of this woman, are God's two laws, written in his Book; the very same that met on David. God has prepared this harlot Rahab in law, or Shem, called Tamar, in gospel or Japheth, to save his two spies. This mystical Babylon is terribly wicked and cruel, having united Simeon and Levi, but the crypt of the convent of the Romish monks, hides the two spies of God. David and the woman, and Benjamin and Judah, or Joseph and Jeruselum, and the Bible, and the two witnesses, are one and the same things, and they are interchangeable terms. The harp of David is upon the willows in this captivity. Will David forget Jerusalem? or will he sing the Lord's song in a strange land? No, no! If from this possessed Saul, as a human king, he is to drive out the evil spirit, it must be according to the laws of the natural king, and it must be done with the artistic skill of musical instruments. This is not the "Lord's song." Let this thought pass for the present.

These thoughts must, of necessity, be transferred to North America to fill up the last side of this triangle according to the types of both the other sides. That which was David, as the two tribes in the literal Babylon, or the word of God, as David among the ten tribes of mystical Babylon, will, in this land, be represented by those collective bodies, making both civil and soul laws, and these are carried into captivity to the "Virgin daughter of Babylon." This virgin daughter, does not claim alliance with the State by statute law, as literal Babylon, or, as mystical Babylon; yet she as virtually unites the two by making a great image, as did her arch-types. The ten horns of mystical Babylon, representing ten kingdoms, are in this "virgin daughter," represented by the ten original tribes or States, that do not come with national Judah. If this virgin daughter talks like a lamb, she acts like a dragon. If she says " governments are by consent of the governed, and religion is free," she sets aside both the laws of Moses and Christ. She has a great image for her God. No use for Moses to say God's covenants are with Abra-Ham. Ham, the father of Canaan, shall serve Japheth in the land of his enlargement. "Thou shalt not covet thy neighbor's servant." No use for Christ to say, " Servants be obedient to your masters. If any man teach otherwise, he is proud, knowing nothing; they have corrupt minds, and are destitute of truth."

Is this virgin daughter of Babylon insincere in all this? No, no, no! They are as sincere as was literal Babylon or mystical Babylon. They feel they are doing God service, and so they are. They are driving Israel to demonstrate the truth that God is king, and that he alone rules in the affairs of men. The Israel of Japheth would never have been settled after the types of the Israel from Shem, had not the "virgin daughter" driven her to do it.

God's form of laws would never have been known without using her as his whip. We cannot refuse to call her brother, because of this captivity. It is not her, but God. It is not done to destroy life, but to save it. When a great light shines upon her, the scales will fall from her eyes, and she will become the great apostle. She will then no longer be Babylon, as the place of confusion, but will be a great worker in rebuilding the temple. If "Hairy Esau standing for the sinful man, in contrast with Red Esau, the natural man, had not driven Jacob, standing for God's double laws, Jacob would never have moved forward. If Esau has his foot upon Jacob's neck, he should not forget that Jacob holds him by the heel, "the hand of man is betwixt the hand and the heel." Jacob will sling out Esau all the world over before it is done.

Let us now proceed in the most concise form to present God's types and God's history in their fulfillment. In order to be concise, we must be dogmatic. It must be taken for granted that the reader is acquainted with Moses who sets the types, and with the prophets who tell how they will be fulfilled, and with the secular history of Israel, which tells when it is done. These are the only things we call Rabbi. To undertake to teach them would require a commentary upon the whole Bible.

The following are the eight types of Christ to build his ark: Two are prophetic, Samuel and Elijah; two are priestly, Isaac and Aaron; two are kingly, Moses and David; and as the seventh combines all of these, he is prophet, priest and king—this one is Joseph. The eighth, made up of the seven, which stands as Noah, the eighth person, is Solomon. The master must come before the world will ever see a greater than Solomon. In splendor and grandure, when the six days working time, is done will the laws of God reign a thousand years as Solomon, which will be the jubilee.

How long will God require to finish this ark? This depends upon what symbol is followed in the count. It will take six days standing for six thousand years, if common time be counted. It will take one hundred and twenty years, which was the age of Moses, if the count is by the jubilee, based upon the square of the seven stars. It will take seventy years, as the age of David, if the count is governed by the number of cycles of Orion. "He maketh the seven stars and Orion." The planet Uranus in modern times is Orion with Job and the prophets. His cycle is complete in eighty-four years. If six thousand be divided by the square of the seven stars as seven by seven—forty-nine, then one year to make the fiftieth to complete the jubilee, the product is one hundred and twenty. This is the age of

Moses, and the length of time which Noah took to build the Ark. If the six thousand be divided by the cycle of Orion which belongs to David the King, not only of the gospel dispensation, but more especially of the representative land in which he was to be restored in the laws for which he stood, which laws are the Ark, or the same as Jerusalem, it will stand six thousand—one hundred and twenty as the Jubilee periods belonging to Moses, which leaves five thousand eight hundred and eighty years. If these be divided by the cycle of Orion, as five thousand eight hundred and eighty by eighty-four, it will give the exact age of David.

Sometimes the summaries have to be added, not only as the jubilee, but also the Sabbatee years. Sometimes they are substracted.

What is true as Dinah with the patriarchs or Paul with the Apostles, neither of which are counted; and what is again true with David and Joseph, both of which are twice counted, is also true in the measures of prophetic times.

In this land in which the literal is fulfilled at every point, it will require only one cycle of Orion or eighty-four years from the first annointing of David as the civil government at Philadelphia, by the Israel of law as twelve tribes, in 1776, to his second annointing by National Judah in 1861 to build Jerusalem or the Ark of Noah. So the seventy weeks of David are here brought down to seventy years from the coming of the moon or the half tribe Manassah, which was the first tribe that came to the original twelve for the second settlement of Israel. This half tribe is Ky—which came in 1791. "Seventy years are determined upon thy people from the going forth of the decree to restore and build Jerusalem." This ended in 1861. The forty years for Israel to journey in the wilderness from the half tribe Ephraim, the same as the first journeyed from the tribe of Judah, or Georgia, began in 1821 and ended in 1861.

The nation to be overthrown, was the nation to re-build Jerusalem. That was to finish the transgression, in both civil and soul laws. They were to annoint the most holy. They were to unseal the book, and make an end of sin. The laws were to meet in this nation, as they had met on the Christ in the Israel from Shem. What a contradiction this is, and yet how exact all is fulfilled? Let us leave these thoughts for the present.

God uniformly has a first, a last and a centre. The six prospective days to build the world and subject it to the laws of the Creator, are divided as follows: The first day as the first thousand years closed with the translation of Enoch. The second day closed with the call of Abraham.

These two thousand years are Monday and Tuesday, in the world's week, and belong to the Anti-deluvian world. The third day closed with the temple of Solomon, with the divine glory filling the house, thus showing how the three days to follow would close with the divine glory to fill the world, and upon which house, not the noise of a hammer by hewing and carving will be heard. The fourth day closed with the coming of the world's moral sun, and agrees with the world's literal sun of the fourth day.

As in the fourth literal day, the light of the moon and the light of the sun, which had been blended together, were separated the one from the other. So the coming of the moral sun at the close of the fourth chilead separated the moon or law from the sun or gospel. The Israels of the moon and sun were also separated. These two days are Wednesday and Thursday, and were given to Shem. The fifth day closed with the deep sleep of the world; as the tenth century was not only the close of the fifth day, but it was the centre of the ten dark centuries, beginning with the sixth and ending with the sixteenth. This was the deep sleep of the world and presaged the coming of the bride from the side of the second Adam, the same as Eve from the side of the first Adam. The sixth day will find the world fitted for the abode of the laws of the second Adam, the same as was typed by the first Adam.

It is now in the Saturday evening of the two days given to Japheth. The days of the last chilead will be shortened, for the elect or law's sake. Were these days not shortened, God's laws would be driven out of the world. Hence the last chilead will not reach its full measure. So far as these days are concerned, they appear to be prospective days, and God may have been six millions of years fitting the earth for the abode of man. Let science go unfettered, and learn from every continent and zone, from every rock and pebble, from every flora and fern, from every footprint, whether mastadon or crawling insect, from every ocean, earth, or twinkling star. In short, let her travel to the outskirts of all things, till the Creator speaks, "Thus far shalt thou go," and the whole will but tend to show the wisdom, power and goodness of the Creator.

The first pair put on trial stand for the two continents, North and South America. This was the prospective place in which they dwelt, whether in literal fact, or no.

The moral world moves in concert with the physical world. As Adam and Eve were one, so with the two continents, North and South America. This oneness of the first Adam not only applies to the laws for which he stood for the double man, but likewise to the double continents. The double laws of the second Adam will not only return as at first given in the first Adam, but the place of starting with the first, is the place of union in the last.

In the garden of Eden, in which dwelt the first Adam, there was a river that parted into four heads. The name of the first was Pison. "This is it that riseth in a land of gold," and is the Missouri river. This is made first because the order follows the movements of Shem, to whom the laws were given, and not that of Japheth.

Shem moved to the East, Japheth to the West. The second river is Gihon. "This is it which goeth through the land of Ethiopia." This is the lower end of the Mississippi river, which from its junction with the Pison, goeth through the land in which Ham was to become the substitute of Canaan in the Israel of Shem.

The name of the third river is Hiddekel, and lieth to the East of Assyria. This is the upper end of the Mississippi, and the same line from West to East is still observed. The fourth and last, as the most remote from the starting point, is Euphrates. This is the Ohio river.

The world has but one continent and one river that answers the description as recorded in Genesis, and at the same time cuts the continent into four grand divisions, agreeing with the four grand divisions of the literal Israel. Two rivers cross each other, from the center of which the heads point to each of the cardinal points, and that is the way in which it goeth. "This is the great valley of the prophet Zich, in which it divided the land from East to West, and half of the mountain removed to the North and half to the South." Mountains, States, tribes or kingdoms, are synomymous terms. As the Euphrates divided the Israel of Shem from the literal Babylon, so the Euphrates, in the Japhetic Israel, sets the boundary between Israel, and the "Virgin daughter of Babylon."

When this river is dried up or broken down, as a partition between Israel and Babylon, it is to prepare the way of the kings of the East; which way is to force the laws of the natural man upon Israel, contrary to the revealed laws of God. This was a necessary result in order to cleanse Israel from her Idols. Were it not so, "God would not have put it into their hearts to agree, and give their power to the beast, or laws of nature, in order to drive Israel to fulfill his word, and demonstrate the meaning of his laws." These thoughts show that the book of Genesis was written in conformity to the present physical arrangement of the world, and is in literal fact no older than Moses. Every part of

Genesis and Job, find their easy and natural application to the history of Israel, from the first Adam who stood to represent the laws of God, down to the triumph of those laws in the second Adam, as husband and bride, as moon and sun, as civil law and soul law. This is not the question now to be considered. As the literal Shem once held possession of the continent of America, so was the land of Shem, as Asia, once joined to America. As he was to loose his literal claim, so have the continents been separated. The literal is up at every point. The seven stars are the seven days of the week; as one of these is broken into fragments, so has God's holy day been broken in the moral world.

The first pair put on test had a positive law of easy comprehension which preceded the test. It was simply to determine whether the compound man would follow the law of the natural, or whether he would follow the law of the supernatural. If he followed the law of the natural, the beast of his nature made of the dust, like the beast, would rule him. If he followed the law of the Creator, then would the divine nature, as the supernatural, rule him. The beasts and birds need no higher law than that of nature to govern them. Had man only had the law of the beast he might have lived and died as a beast, in which the strongest would have ruled. As man was something more than the beast, having not only a body possessing all the passions and appetites of the beast, but likewise a soul, divine in its nature and as capable of suffering or enjoying as the body, and not only these distinct natures, but an organism that gave the power of reasoning that stood as the agent to keep up communication between these distinct natures, the Creator gave him a law differing from that given to the beast. This law he violated, choosing to follow the law of the beast. This act has followed his posterity, and all alike choose to follow the law of the beast. Eve standing for the soul half of man's nature, said, "The serpent tempted and I did eat." Adam, the body, said, "The woman gave me." As these followed the beast and not the laws of God, being yet natural and supernatural, that thus begotten in the act is called the "Nahash" or serpent. It is the rule in these things that the act of the parent belongs to the child. If Isaac, "the Christ, trembles exceedingly" in turning "Hairy Jacob" to smooth Jacob, or rather to "Wrestling Israel," the act pertains to the subject and not to the one setting the sign. We say Hairy Jacob, because he was made to put on the hairy gloves of Esau, to show that by nature he was as hairy as Esau.

The "exceeding trembling" is the act of the subject in

the new birth. It is not "the Christ," as Isaac that trembles, though the act is applied to Isaac. If Sarah laughs at the promise of the birth of Isaac and then asserts, "I laughed not," there is no contradiction in it. Isaac is the soul, when that is born it laughs, and yet it does not laugh. It does not laugh derisively as a natural man or from the pleasure of the outer, but from the pleasing emotions of the inner man. These thoughts are enough to show that the act of the parent is given to show the nature of the thing begotten. That which was begotten in the double act of Adam and Eve, as natural and supernatural is represented by the "Nahash." That is, it has a divine nature, being the offspring of divine parentage, but no divine power by which it could overcome the infirmity of its fallen nature. The world could never become a "living soul" by following the laws of this offspring, resulting from the act of Adam and Eve. But God had determined it should become a "living soul," and that in doing this he would use this "Nahash," this proclivity to evil, as his servant, in bringing this about. Obedience to the laws of the Maker is that that will make the world a "living soul" to its dead body, as a physical world. This obedience includes both civil and soul laws.

In the second test act of God with man, it was with the three sons of Noah, standing for the three continents of Asia, Africa and Europe. The test this time does not turn upon a law of easy comprehension, to see whether man will follow the beast, or the law of God, as in the first instance, but it turns upon the point of how shall the infirmity of the first pair be overcome. It was not to see whether the soul or church, would cover itself with "fig-leaves" instead of the laws of the Creator, or whether the world would be sober or drunk. It was already drunk, as Noah was drunk. Means were to be devised by which to sober it. The only thing that could sober it was the laws of the Maker. These laws were very complex in their character, and the maker intended to write them in a book, and then write them again in his book of nature, in which nations, and kingdoms, and cycles and churches, should be their exponent.

While the test in the first pair turned upon the observance of a law already given and of easy comprehension, that of the second turned upon the power of capacity to understand a complex law when demonstrated. Those of Noah's sons, (or if the reader pleases) the world's sons, that gave evidence of having overcome the "Nahash," or inclination to follow the beast, or natural, were the ones to whom the laws were to be given. As Ham, the youngest son, looked with indifference upon a naked and drunken world, he was still a beast, and in this sense stands as the literal representative of the "Nahash," begotten by the first pair. Two thousand years from Adam finds him the beast at first begotten by Adam and Eve. If he had gained nothing above the beast during this time, and had learned nothing from his "Father Noah, a preacher of righteousness," it was the evidence that so far as he was concerned the world would remain naked and drunk, till the day of doom, and he would never cover that nakedness by following the laws of the Maker. In the person of Ham, the youngest son of Noah, the "Nahash" of Adam and Eve assumes bodily form as the literal representative of the natural man to pursue the laws of nature. Such is his nature arising from the ascendency of the beast, that he could never be made conformable to the laws of the Maker if left to his own powers of tracing cause and sequence, or type and anti-type, in the demonstration. Still, he is not a beast, in the full sense of that term. He is the thing begotten by the natural and supernatural, as Adam and Eve; if not in very deed, he is so regarded by God's symbols, which makes it very deed, and that he is possessed with a soul, as is the other brothers, will fully appear before we are done. Were he wholly a beast, no good reason could be assigned for imposing it upon Shem and Japheth to make him a servant of tribute.

Ham is in a double sense a "Servant of servants." God made promise that the "Seed of the woman should bruise the serpent's head," but that the serpent, or "Nahash," should "Bruise his heel." The meaning of which is, God would use that inclination to follow nature to drive that same nature to demonstrate that he alone had the right to rule. That is, he would make the antagonism of that nature. kill itself. While in the contest his own laws would be bruised; yet in the end they should conquer. This should be not only in the "Begotten Son," but in a nation bringing forth both the first born son, and the begotten son. Thus he would use the "Nahash," or Ham, as his servant of the two laws, making his servants. As in all things, the literal is up with the symbolic, the literal Ham was to be a literal servant of tribute.

The other brothers who walked backwards to cover the nakedness of their father; by that symbolic act, showed that they had risen above the law of the beast, which felt no concern about whether the world was drunk or sober.

By this act they showed that they had learned to feel for the infirmities of others; and reason, if not revelation, had made some impression upon them. This test act showed a capacity of comprehending what the beast never could comprehend, and that they could understand complex laws when demonstrated.

What now are the symbolic laws which the three brothers represent. Ham is the literal representative of that class who follow the laws of nature in both the natural and supernatural man. Shem stands as the Israel with the law of the body as given by God, and a literal law of the soul; Japheth is the law of God for the soul, and the law of nature for the body. Shem and Japheth jointly are God's laws for both body and soul, civil and church. These are what God will have, and it must begin with Japheth.

In bringing all things back to the original, it was "The earth that helped the woman." The woman is the Bible. It will be seen that the British Isles, are "the earth." She stood as the gospel Judah of Japheth from between whose feet the lawgiver was to come. The two Islands of England and Scotland are as the two continents of North and South America. If to these Ireland be added, they then represent Asia, Africa and Europe. She is the world in miniature. When God's laws are established in that unity for which they were designed, the single continent of Australia stands to represent this unity.

"The book of the generation of Adam" is the book of the generation of God, to fill up his world's week. The literal generations are the symbols of civil governments. These are called "Sons of God," because they represent his laws down the line of Israel's history. When these mix with human laws, they mingle with the "seed of men." When these meet in human laws for State and church, according to the types, then is the geneology complete.

Eve is the only woman used to represent the church until the covenants made with Abraham. She stands to represent the soul, rather than the church of the soul. Sarah, the wife of Abraham, is the law of gospel, or the soul, in contrast with Hager the cermonial law. Rebecca, the wife of Isaac, is the gospel church; nor does she arise till all the prophetic signs are fulfilled and all the times are measured for her to come forth. The literal acts of the literal Israel are the symbols of gospel Israel. Rebecca, the church of gospel, does not rise till after the forty-two months captivity of mystical Babylon closes after the "breaking of the day," or reformation.

She rises at the same place that Sarai is changed to Sarah, or Jacob to Israel. This is not done till Jacob starts back to his "father's house," or laws, and crosses the brook Jabbok with his family and enters "Red Esau's land," and then recrosses it to "wrestle with the angel." The church of Rebecca does not rise till, like Isaac, " meeting her in the field;" preaching the word of God, begins in the field. Every literal act of these "Sons of God" is a speaking prophecy and must find their appropriate places in history. These acts are given to fix the points from which to measure the times of the prophets. The literal acts are the skeleton, or Moses. The prophets tell how to put the flesh upon it, or to clothe it. No use for one to rise from the dead and tell a different story. God always did intend at his appointed time to be understood.

By measure hath he measured the times. and by number hath he numbered the times, and he doth not move nor stir till the said measure be fulfilled." Esdeas. "Days were to speak, and years teach wisdom. As these move forward they turn the pages of the book, and man is only asked to look and see, and learn the truth. As God saved Noah, the eighth person, a preacher of righteousness," so he means to save the world. He means to save Solomon, the eighth and last and highest type of God.

Solomon has wives, and concubines enough to cover the world. God will do this by his own laws. All shall know the Lord," David, as civil law, was restored to rule at the rise of the twelve tribes as the United States. This was David, with seven wives, standing for seven churches."

This was the first annointing of David in the gospel Israel, given to Japheth in the land of his enlargement. David is again annointed by national Judah, and the Bathsheba, among the seven churches, is pointed out. This Bathsheba comes of the tribe of Judah, in national Judah, and at her head stands Andrew as the first Apostle, who was born of Judah.

In order to find the truth, God's symbolic characters must be tracked from Adam till to-day. In order to find David as the representative of God's laws in the Israel of Japheth, the same lines must be observed that were given in the "bond-woman," or Israel of Shem, that brought forth the literal David. The raising up of David and sitting him upon the throne, " is the raising up of the laws of God for which David stood and seating them upon the throne. If the literal David was through the first born of Judah's twins, as Phares as the political government, he will be, through the first born of the gospel Israel, given to Judah or Japheth. If the literal David came through Rahab and Ruth, in the literal, he will come through that wing in the gospel, for which they stand in their symbolic character, when applied to Judah, as gospel, who stands for the one tribe to remain to the house of David."

Each circle of the several symbols must be considered before the exact sense can be reached. Like the celestial heavens they move as an orb within an orb. The grand division is followed by subdivisions, all of which are given to get the sense.

Let us now track these symbols as they apply to the Israel of law given to Shem, and to gospel Israel given to Japheth in Europe. These two wings have the same ending, and a new start was made at the rise of the United States, as the land in which Japheth was "enlarged over Shem." The twelve original colonies of this land were the Israel of law. We say twelve, "Simeon and Levi are brethern," and stand as one in this demonstrative Israel. These are simply Carolina in this explanatory land. Another twelve, or eleven and two half tribes are cut off, which brings Jacob to his fathers laws, in a South land. These will tell the watchmen what the hour of the night; these will tell what God thinks of all human laws, whether in Church or State; these will show that the land has never had one accidental President, and that one has never died only by God's appointment. If they will tell every man what God thinks of every important vote he ever cast, let the reader remember it is not the doings of the feeble and obscure writer, who has no skill nor power to do anything. All we can do is simply to look at God's facts as he has made them, which it seems to us any thinking mind can do as well as we.

If they shall show to every one that there is no "man that sinneth not," it will only confirm the truth of the declaration of Solomon.

The line of political governments from Adam, representing the body, or civil law of the body, is through Cain. The line of the soul, or church of the soul from Eve, is through Abel, or through Seth, who came in the place of Abel.

Adam, is the anti-deluvian world; Cain is the Israel of law given to Shem. To the offering of Cain as "the fruits of the ground," God found no fault, saying, "If thou doest well shalt not thou be accepted." The same was true of the Israel of law. Cain killed his brother for the simple reason that his sacrifice was received with approbation, whereas Cain's did not get the approbation. The same is true of the Israel of law, who killed the world's Abel. Cain was a tiller of the soil, so were they; Cain was cast out, so were they. Cain ceased to till the soil, and became a trafficer, so have they. God set a mark on Cain; God set a mark in the flesh of the Israel of law. Cain said, "Whoever findeth me will slay me." The Israel of law has been slain in all lands, and suffered more than any people upon the earth. The name of Cain has become a by-word of reproach. He will Jew you, is a by-word of reproach. God said, " Let Cain live ; whoever killeth him shall have vengeance taken upon him sevenfold." The Israel of law for which Cain stands, like the law for which they stand, are God's " burning bush." They cannot die. They will live to see every persecutor they ever had blotted out of existence. They move with the law for which they stand. They are Benjamin to Joseph : " Benjamin shall dwell in safety all the day long, and in the evening he shall divide the spoil." While they represent law, Joseph is both law and gospel. Egypt, Babylon, Greece, Rome, the ten hours, will all die, but this Cain will live. While he is of Shem, or the bond-woman, and it is his business to carry the law into all the world; Japheth must carry the gospel. These shall come together, both literally and symbolically.

There is a double trinity in Cain : These are Cain, Cainan and Tubalcain. These are the natural man as Cain. God's law of the natural man, given in the land of Canaan as "The fruits of the ground Tubalcain," the laws of God mixing up with the laws of men. Cain, Cainan, Tubalcain, stand the natural or wicked man. The literal man Cainan, as the servant in the land of Canaan, &c. When Cain as the Israel of law was cast out, and the law for which these stood mingled with " the seed of men," they jointly became "Tubalcain and his sister Naamah." The literal account is Cain cast out begat a son whose name was Enoch, and builded a city, and called it by his son's name." The first change which the gospel of Judah made in the civil government of Rome, in which Cain, or the Israel of law, was " cast out," was in Constantine. The city builded by Constantine was Constantinople, and he is the Enoch of Cain. Irad, is the empire of Rome, divided into East and West; Mehujael, is the West broken into ten kingdoms, holding one form of religion ; Methusael is Protestant England, separating from Rome, and Lamech is the United States, as the Israel of law in Japheth, settled after the order of the " old estates," as given to Shem. " This Lamech was the literal Union, first formed at the literal Philadelphia in this land.

This Israel had not only to " fly upon the shoulders of the Philistines to the West"—that is, sail in ships—but it had to journey forty years in the wilderness, the same as the Israel of Shem. This journey is from the tribe of Judah or Georgia, as the tribe at which it is said "Lear left bearing," and is the last tribe of the first settlement as the Israel of law given to Japheth.

In this count, if the count begins with the civil or body, it ends with the church or soul. If it begins with the church it ends with the civil, and both must end in forty years, by an organization at Philadelphia, as husband and bride, as it was the church among the seven of St. John, at Philadelphia, that "held the key of David."

This Lamech, as the Israel of law, made up of twelve tribes given to Japheth in the land of his "enlargement," took two wives. The church had existed in two forms, and he granted toleration to both. The one wife as Adah, standing for the ceremonial law of Shem, had two sons, as two forms of civil government. She bare Jabal "that kept flocks," and Jubal that played on "musical instruments." The Israel of Shem was first patriarchal, and then it became kingly, not by the law of God, but by the will of man, which said, "Governments are by the consent of the governed." This change took place when the law of God had been perfected in the seventh representative head of law as judges, and it became Jubal or kingly, as Saul, the first king, by the will of man. David, with his "musical instrument," playing before Saul, is man's form of laws. The form of God is Jabal or the patriarchal form, as he entered his "solemn protest" against the departure from that form as his civil law of the body. He stands pledged to have a nation to take the kingdom. Elias restores all things. The protest against man's king, is the protest against the musical instrument to drive out the evil spirit that governs man. If the musical instrument is required to gather the people to the house of God, it is the king of man. God intends his own laws shall do this without any help from human kings. "Forsake not the assembling of yourselves," is the word of God. It is enough to know that God said it. As God granted the king, in accordance to the weakness of man's nature, so he granted the musical instrument in accordance with the weakness of the same nature. Neither the one, nor the other, will be needed, or even asked for, when the demonstration is finished; but God will be the king. When this is done, the saying of David will be fulfilled, "Let the people praise Thee; let all the people praise Thee." This time is not yet.

The other wife of Lamech stands to represent Japheth, or the gospel Israel in Rome. This wife was named Zillah, and she bare "Tubalcain and his sister, Naamah." This wife came up when Cain, or Shem, or the Israel of law, was cast out, and she came in the union of civil and church laws in Constantine. The literal Naamah, the wife of Solomon, was the line to bring forth the Christ, upon whom the laws of

God met. The laws of God to bring forth David, must follow the same line.

This wife Zillah is the representative of a forcible union between church and State. The law of the church leads the law of the State the same as Eve led Adam, and the State wields the force to bring men to the standard of morals which the church establishes. When this is the condition, whether it be with Zillah, or Tubalcain and his sister, Naamah," in Rome, or in this land of Lamech, "They compass land and sea to make our proselytes and keep their sentinels upon the lookout to hunt souls."

"Tubalcain was the inventor of everything in brass and iron, and thus stands as the opposite of the sturdy habits of Patriarchal Jabal, that kept flocks and tilled the soil. This Lamech told these two wives he had a double work to do; he had to slay a "man, and a young man ; that he would slay the man to his wounding and the young man to his hurt." That is, as the Israel of God to bring forth his own laws, he had to slay the kingly form of government that came up in the Israel of Shem, which substituted the one man power for the law of God. As the Israel of Japheth, or gospel given by Judah, left that gospel and united both the civil and soul laws in the man of sin that crept into the temple of God," he would slay him. Lamech had to slay both departures from the double laws of God, whether as the civil king in Shem as soul, or whether as both the civil and soul king as in Rome. The substitutes for these are Moses and Christ. This Lamech slayed the kingly form, or the one man power, with the twelve first tribes as the Israel of law. These began with Reuben as the Exodox or Virginia, and ended with Georgia or Judah, in the first settlement in this land, and this whole lot of children was Leah's; all included between the first and last, were Leah's, as the first and last were hers. This one man power as the "Divine right of kings" followed the law of the beast in that he forced laws upon Israel in which they had no voice. This mark of the beast in the first instance of slaying a man was presented by George III, in the "Stamp act." It required a seven years war for Lamech to slay the old king; he is as old as Egypt. The young man, as a union of civil and soul laws, is only half as old as the old man, as he come into being after the coming of gospel by Judah. This young man, as Ephraim, representing ten tribes, built "golden heifers" in the literal Israel. The same young man standing for ten tribes as Ephraim built golden heifers in Rome, by the sale of indulgencies. Both of these, as type and anti-type, represented the one-half of the first Israel. Ten tribes of this Japhetic Israel of law, North of

Reuben, in the first settlement, have again built "golden heifers;" these have united State and church, and made a great image. None dare teach either Moses or Christ. Will Lamech slay this young man? It will be to his hurt. He will slay him with that Israel that stands for both law and gospel. The first and the last, are the two of Rachel's in this second settlement, Joseph and Benjamin.

In this second settlement, the two sons of Rachel, that stand as the summaries of laws that were first set up at Philadelphia, after forty years from the last tribe of Judah, are now "the first and the last," as was Reuben and Judah, in the first settlement. It will require Jacob moving as "God the Holy Ghost" to get Rachel, a seven years service, the same as it required seven years war, in the first instance, to get both Leah and Rachel, jointly. These two as wives to God's laws must be separated. Rachel is what is wanting; nothing but Rachel God will have. She is the word of God; she is not only Moses, with twelve patriarchs, as law standing as Benjamin, but she is Joseph, as twelve apostles, to add the soul to the body. The lawgivers, to bring this Rachel, must come out of Judah in this land, the same as the Christ or David upon whom they met, came of Judah.

The tribe of Georgia is Judah. This tribe, in the first settlement of this Israel of law, extended to the Mississippi river. The two tribes which came of this Judah as Alabama and Mississippi, make the literal feet of the literal Judah. While the head of the church must come of Judah, the civil head must come from "between his feet." Let this pass for the present. The main point to be observed is, that the twelve original colonies of this land as the restored Israel given to Japheth, stand for the Lamech in the line of the civil law from Adam. The line of the church through Seth must be brought up and see if it coincides with the civil line at the same point as the Lamech to bring forth the Noah to save the world.

The following are the names of the generations from Adam through Seth; Adam, Seth, Enos, Cainan, Mahalaleel, Jared, Enoch, Methuselah, Lamech. Adam, the anti-deluvian world; Seth, the ceremonial law given to Shem; Enos, the gospel by Christ; Cainan, that gospel united with the civil yet subordinate to the civil under Constantine; Mahalaleel, the gospel divided between Greek and Latin, and superior to the State; Jared, the reformation, breaking away from the State; Enoch, Diocesian Episcopal Ruth. that followed Naamah the mother-in-law; Methusalah, the dissentees, as Orpah, "that kissed the mother-in-law and turned back," or became congregational; Lamech, the church of

John Wesley, which came between the feet of Judah, holding with both Ruth and Orpha, and organizing a church with a Bishop as the head, and yet teaching for the soul "Ye must be born again."

This church of Mr. Wesley, as Lamech, in this land, dates from the tribe of Judah, forty years to Philadelphia. Oglethorpe settled in Georgia in 1733. On the 4th day of July, 1773, the church of Mr. Wesley was first organized at the literal Philadelphia; Mr. Wesley came over to this Israel and to the tribe of Judah in 1736. On the 4th day of July, 1776, the two lines which meet in Lamech from Adam, at Philadelphia as civil and soul laws, met each forty years from Judah at Philadelphia. Each of these are the seventh, to agree with David the seventh son of Jessee. These two are Joseph and Benjamin, the summaries of God's laws. As in the acts of the literal Jacob in entering Esau's land, Rachel and her children came in the rear of Leah and her children; so in this land those that stand for Rachel, were forty years in the rear of the last tribe of Leah, as Judah or Georgia. All the other churches of this land are Leah's (as will be seen,) save that one that dates from Judah to Philadelphia, in the first settlement.

At the birth of Benjamin, Rachel died. As a tribe in this land Benjamin is the "Lone Star, Texas," and the literal Israel moves not more uniformly with the law of Moses, in the history of the world, than does this literal tribe in this land move with the law of the land, as first set up at Philadelphia.

If the literal Jerusalem was built between the tribes of Judah and Benjamin, as the two tribes at which Leah "left bearing, and at which Rachel died." So will it be seen that the laws of God for which the literal Jerusalem stood, are again brought back in this national Judah, between the tribes of Judah and Benjamin, as the last of the first settlement of the Israel of law, and then the last of the second settlement of the Israel of both law and gospel.

Joseph, to whom the "birthright is given among the sons of Jacob," stands for the church, and at whose birth it was said, "Send me away to my country and my people," was the church of John Wesley, first sent away from England as "the earth that helped the woman," and was first set up at Philadelphia. This church was sent away because in this land it was organized into a different form from that held by the land from which it was sent. At the second sending of this Joseph in this land at the end of twenty-four hundred years, according to the reading of the seventy, the church of John, the forerunner, as John Wesley, whose mother was Elizabeth, agreeing with the literal types, which Elizabeth was the head of the Church of England. As the literal John brought his disciple Andrew to Christ, so the church of John Wesley was brought by Andrew in the person of Bishop James Andrew, who was born of the tribe of Judah or Georgia in this land. The accounts concerning Seth are doubled. It is intentional. One accounts says: "Seth begat Enos, then began men to call upon the name of the Lord." It has been seen that Seth in the line of gospel descent stands for the ceremonial law, and Enos for the gospel of Christ, whose first Apostle was Andrew. If in this land that which stands as Lamech, or the church set up at Philadelphia, it will represent the church of Wesley. If Enos be taken as the son of this Seth, it is the church of God in this land founded upon Andrew out of Judah, the same as the gospel given in Shem, or the Israel of law.

Two things are to be done, God's forms of civil law and church law, and both are to be in agreement with these as given in the literal Israel. The "pillow of fire and cloud" guided the literal Israel not more certainly than their acts guide the Israel of Japheth in this land of his enlargement over Shem.

Other symbolic characters must be applied to Israel's history before coming to the tribes of this land. The literal Jacob was the father of the literal Israel in Asia or in Canaan as the land of Shem. The literal Jacob is the literal character to symbolize the movements of "God the Holy Ghost," proceeding from the father and the son representing Abraham and Isaac. It was in Isaac the seed were to be called to fill the covenants set with Abraham. Isaac had two sons, Jacob and Esau. Every man born into the world is by nature Hairy Esau. As such he has a natural law for the body and a natural religion. Jacob must in every man twice supplant this Esau. "These two times has my brother supplanted me," is the language of Esau. Smooth Jacob must supplant Esau in his natural law, that says kill, steal, covet, &c. "Wrestling Israel" must supplant Hairy Esau in his natural or outward religion. Man must get religion, and then do religion. This is the law of God, and this is the theological part of the subject, which belongs not to the enquiry in hand. Esau, the first born son of Isaac, was entitled to the literal Israel, but Jacob got that. Red Esau got first into this land of North America, as the place of the Japhetic Israel, and Jacob has driven him from that. Esau is to gospel Israel as Ham to Shem and Japheth, with this difference in their natures:—

While Ham can be made obedient to the laws of God,

that "man shall live in the sweat of his face," the love of the "quiver and the bow" in Red Esau, is too great for him to conform to this law of the Creator. The normal relation of Ham as a servant acting in obedience to the laws of God, has given him possession of the land of Red Esau, and Esau is in a fair way to be exterminated. Not only will the red man be driven out, but Hairy Esau, as the man that lives by the sword, will also be driven out, by Jacob, moving as God the Holy Ghost.

The symbolic character of Jacob must follow that of Isaac. As Isaac is the Christ the Son offered, Jacob must follow Isaac. As the son was offered at the close of law given to Shem, Jacob must find his correspondents in gospel Israel given to Japheth. As there were two settlements to make in the Japhetic Israel—once as law to agree with Moses, and once as gospel to agree with Christ, when the twelve apostles were to sit on "twelve thrones judging the twelves tribes"—the symbolic acts of the literal Jacob must be twice used in making the settlement. When Jacob left his father's house, and camped for the night, he saw a ladder that reached from "earth to heaven," upon which the angels of God ascended and descended. When he awoke, he erected a pillow of stones and poured oil upon it, as a note of attention, that there was a symbolic meaning in the act. This act symbolized that the "bond-woman," or ceremonial law, would be sent back to her mistress in the gospel dispensation, which was done in the seven sacraments of Rome.

These carried people to heaven, by the ladder of Jacob, or by doing things. These ceremonies in the Gospel Israel, lasted until the time came for the day to break at the reformation. After Jacob had gathered up his family in the service of Laban, and started to return to his father's house, he crossed the brook Jabbok, and then recrossed alone; and there came an angel and wrestled with him. Jacob wrestled the long night, symbolizing the long night when the woman or law of God was hid in the convent of the monks of Rome. He cried, "let me go to the day: the day breaketh,"—symbolizing the reformation, when the woman would begin to shed her light. He got a blow upon his thigh in the contest, and halted upon it. This is the inquisition when the joints of the victim were dislocated. The angel asked, "What is thy name?" "My name is Jacob." The reply was "Thou art no longer Jacob, but Israel." It was John Wesley who came into Red Esau's land as did Jacob, a member of the church of England, the same as Jacob was of the ceremonial law, and who came into the tribe of Judah as the last of the tribes that came from England and then returned to "wrestle with the angel," as did Jacob, and in the wrestle said he felt his heart "strangely warmed." This then is the place at which Jacob was changed to Israel. It is the same place at which Saria, the law of gospel, was changed to Sarah. It was here that Isaac, the child of promise, as the soul, was born again. This is the place for the rise of Rebecca, the gospel church. It began with preaching in the field, the place where God the son, as Isaac, met Rebecca "coming in the field." This was the time of the release of Sarah by the king of Egypt, in gospel given to Japheth, the same as in law given to Shem. Sarah was restored to Abraham, with all that Abraham had, at the rise of the Israel of law given to Japheth; Sarah, the law of gospel, is twice captured, once by Egypt, and once by Abimilech. Rebecca, the church of gospel, is once captured, and that is by Abimilech. We shall find who this Abimilech is before we are done. Turning to the prophet Daniel, "How long shall the sanctuary and the host be trodden under foot?" And he said unto, "Two thousand and three hundred days: then shall the sanctuary be cleansed." The translation of the LXX read it twenty-four hundred in place of twenty-three hundred, (Bishop Newton.) No point is made from which to date the prophecy, hence it must date from the time it was given. Dr. A. Clark dates it at 553 B. C.; Calmet at 557. This is near enough. The cleansing of the sanctuary not only had respect to the cleansing of the heart, but also to the organization of the church, in which none but the Levites should take down the ark and set it up. The sanctuary had to be doubly cleansed, both at twenty-three hundred years, and also at twenty-four hundred, according to the double reading of the original. A day is a year. Dating the prophecy at 556 B. C. or between Drs. Clark and Calmet, it would end in 1744, i. e. 556 by 1744—2300. The year 1744 was the time of the first conference ever held by the Rev. J. Wesley, with six preachers, at the cannon foundary in London. This was Melchisede, priest of the most high God, born without father or mother. Not by any line of procreation, but by the power of an endless life. The sanctuary needed a second cleansing in this land, because Mr. Wesley did not conform in outward laws to Moses and Christ in his organization of the church. There were two defects in his church. These were pointed out in the second cleansing in this land at the end of 2400 years, or in 1844. Until the civil law for the body and church law for the soul, both harmonize upon the divine plan, there can be no peace. The nearer they approach, the more desperate the contest. Let these thoughts pass for the present. Let us now turn to the literal acts of the literal Judah of whom "the Christ came," and apply these to gospel Israel given to Japheth. While the literal Israel as Shem, is represented by Benjamin, gospel Israel is Judah. Christ came of Judah and gave the gospel. This gospel church was named "Tamer," after the only daughter, the literal David, the type of the gospel church, had. When the ten persecutions of the dragon of Pagan Rome had well nigh driven this Tamer out of the world, Judah standing as the law of the church, appointed Er to keep up the succession. This Er was wicked and God slew him. Judah then appointed Onan to keep up the succession, and he would not. Tamer had the promise of the other and last son of Judah as the law of the gospel. This son was Shelah, but she never got him. As the literal keeps up with the symbolic, Shelah turned monk in the person of Anthony, the first Monk, about the close of the third or the beginning of the fourth century. (Historians are not agreed in facts.) Judah who stood as the head of the church of gospel, turned politician in the person of Constantine, and ordered an election of Bishops, and converted Tamer into an harlot. The election did not turn upon those most worthy to fill the office, but upon those who could furnish the finest tables, and the most luxuriant dishes. None can read Gibbon in reference to this election, but will be struck at once with the saying of Judah, "Take this kid to the harlot Tamer."

God never leaves himself without a witness. If the churches' historians refuse to testify to his truth as set in his types, he will make the stones speak. Skeptics are often better witnesses of God's truth than are those who set themselves to be its defenders. The messenger to bear the kid returned and said, "There was no harlot there;" Judah said, "There was a harlot there." This question has been debated in the world from that day to this. Did Tamer become a harlot, or did she not? The types preceding this will settle it in favor of Judah, that there was a harlot there. Elijah stands as Christ, and Elisha, upon whom he threw his mantle, is the twelve Apostles. Elijah found Elisha plowing with twelve yoke of oxen, and he with the twelfth. These twelve are one patriarch and one apostle that make one yoke. Elisha turned back and sacrificed one yoke with their instruments. This one yoke stood for the whole twelve. These were Dinah among the patriarchs, and Paul among the Apostles. As this yoke stood for the twelve, so Elisha stood for the whole. When the one yoke was sacrificed the whole was lost. Gospel Judah, whose business it was to speak from the ground, like the blood of Abel or the Master, put off his grave cloths and changed the law of Abel into that of Cain, and in this relation begat two illegitimate sons, by the harlot Tamer, in the persons of Phares and Zarah, or the Latin and Greek churches. As the literal brothers struggled to see which should be born first, so did these brothers struggle up to the ninth century to see which should be born first. The one as Zarah, or the Greek's, that seemed as if he should be born first, and made heavy threats against his brother, was at last preceded by his brother Phares, or the Latins, who holding his seat at Rome thundered against his brother at Constantinople, and ex-communicated the patriarch and his whole patriarchate. The line of God's succession to bring forth the literal David was through Phares, the first born son of Judah; so in gospel given to Japheth, it must be through the Latin's, as Phares, the first born of Judah's twins.

This church, as Tamer, stands as Rahab to literal Israel. It was Rahab that saved the twelve spies in the literal Israel; only two of which were needed to stand for the twelve. It is the Latins or Western church that was represented by ten kingdoms, as Goths, Osthagoths, Franks, Allmen, &c., that stand for ten of these spies as literal governments, while the two that she hid in the crypt of the convent, are Joshua and Caleb, as Old and New Testament. This Tamer, or Rahab, or Naamah, or Naomi is the mother of Ruth and Orpah. The line of God's succession is through Ruth, as the Church of England, that followed the mother-in-law. The gospel Israel, as Judah, in the land of Japheth in Europe, make the feet of that Judah from between which the law-giver was to come. The political feet of this Judah are the seventh head of England as Cromwell, and the seventh of Rome as Napoleon Bonaparte.

Between the tragical ending of Charles of England and the Bourbons of France, under the Jacobins, at which times the scepter left Judah, in Europe the Israel of law in the land of Japheth's enlargement, as the United States, arose. So between the feet of gospel Judah, headed by Ruth or Elizabeth, as Episcopal, and Congregational Orpah as the Puritan Cromwell, standing for all the Congregational churches, came the church of Wesley for this land with a Bishop for its head. The law-giver was to come from "between the feet of Judah," standing for gospel Israel.

Several other lines in God's succession deserve to be considered. The smallest amount of light required to set the prophetic times, is all that can be indulged in this synopsis. It was Simeon, the second son of Jacob, standing for the second or gospel Israel, that united with Levi as the church that "dug down a wall" that God had set up between the two, and joined them together. Simeon and Levi when joined together are always "cruel." When Dinah, the church, conformed the Shichemites to gospel, which was symbolized by having them circumcised, these cruel brothers took advantage of their soreness, or of the doctrines of the gospel, "Thou shalt not kill," "Blessed are the merciful," and slew them, saying, "Shall they corrupt our sister?" Shall they corrupt our church? Those whom they slew are the blood of "Righteous Abel speaking from the ground." These cruel brothers are still united, and "Abel is speaking from the ground." The souls under the altar are still crying, "How long, O Lord, before our blood shall be avenged." The time for the vindication of God's martyred witnesses, and laws draweth near. Rest a little longer. The God who gave them, is where he was, and there he will remain. The ship is not without its pilot, nor the stage without the driver.

Job is the image of God's church drawn by God himself. It would be a pleasant task to show who his three friends are, that desired to mend his way of serving God, and show the four times they reply to Job, when they are older than Job, or pagan friends; and also the four replies they make, when Job is older than they, or when the laws that make Job are finished. As there is no difficulty in doing this, or in telling who his fourth or last friend Elihu is, and as it does not have an important bearing upon the main question of telling that symbolic sense as the representatives of laws which God attached to the twelve tribes, we pass by Job, with a simple enquiry into his seven sons. The seven sons of Job are the seven literal acts or characters of God to bring forth his form of civil law for the head, or body of man, taken in its collective sense; these are Abraham, Isaac, Jacob, Israel, divided by the sale of Joseph, Israel united by Joseph in Egypt, with Joseph exalted to power; Moses, the law-giver of Israel for both body and soul; judges of whom Joshua was first to represent the whole. These are the seven heads to make the law for collective Israel.

When Israel left the law of these seven, it was under "solemn protest," yet it was to bring forth another seven, of which the first seven were the type to give God's law for the bride or church. These seven are, Saul, David, Solomon, Israel, divided with the two tribes; Benjamin and Judah, in captivity, to Babylon, the same as Joseph was in Egypt; Israel, exalted in Babylon by Daniel, interpreting the dreams of the king as did Joseph, and Israel allowed to re-build the temple the same as Joseph's brethern came to him. The sixth head is Christ agreeing with Moses, and the seventh are the apostles, of whom Andrew was first. These twice seven counted heads are one, and they are God's forms of laws for the double man of his creation. Nothing less than these will make David. Each is the seventh, and the union of the two will stand as Solomon, the last type of God's laws, and as the " eighth of the seven." There were fourteen civil judges of the literal Israel giving to these twice seven heads one judge each. These judges were presidents, chosen by the people according to the law of Moses. These fourteen judges were the following: Joshua, Othdal, Ehu, Shamgar, Barck, Gideon, Abimilech, Tola, Jair, Jeptha. Ibson, Elon, Abdon, Samson. These are the fourteen civil presidents of the Israel of law, which gives one judge to the twice counted seven heads. These leave out Deborah, Samuel, Eli and sons, because they are representatives of the church and of her action in Israel. Let it be observed that the first is Joshua, and the seventh is Abimilech, and the last is Samson. The seventh is uniformly the turning point in Israel's history. Let us now track these through Pagan Rome, Papal Rome, England and the United States, as the Israel of law given to Japheth. Pagan Rome swallowed up the Israel of Shem, and as she belonged to Japheth or gospel Israel, the count must come through her. What has been her forms of laws and who is the bride to her? The civil heads of Pagan Rome, were kings, consuls, dictators, decemvere's triumvinis, heathen, emperors, under the Cæsars; Christian emperors, under Constantine. In the days of St. John, five of these heads had fallen or passed away.

The apostle said "One is, and one is yet to come, and when he cometh he must continue for a short space." The sixth head was the one that then was, which was the Imperial head under Nero Cæsar. The one to come, was the Christian head under Constantine, who united the seventh head of gospel with the sixth of Rome, and thus made the seventh. The Christian head continued a short space, because in Julian, the nephew of Constantine, he apostatised from the faith of his uncle. As the churches' head was revived again, it became "the eighth that was of the seven," and Papal Rome stands as the bride to Pagan Rome. What now are the seven heads of "Papal Rome?" Rome divided between East and West. The West broken into ten kingdoms, granting civil powers to the Pope. "The little horn that plucked up three civil powers by the roots." The Pope for the first time placing the purple upon Pepin of France.

The Pope placing the crown upon Charles the V of Spain at the time, for the day to break, or at the reformation. The protestant head of England, tearing away from the Pope in the reign of Elizabeth—Napoleon Bonaparte assuming authority over the Pope of Rome. These seven heads are represented by the literal seven mountains upon which Rome was built, while the seven of Pagan Rome are represented by the seven sons of Japheth. Henry the VIII of England, acted the double part of Rome, and Ruth, to represent the action of his two daughters, Mary and Elizabeth.

That Elizabeth is chosen instead of her father to represent Protestant England, is shown by the act of God in the settlement of the two tribes in this land of the literal, bearing the names of the daughters, Mary and Elizabeth.

What have been the seven heads of England, which was separated from Rome to make the feet of Judah or Gospel, given to Japheth, the same as the two tribes. Benjamin and Judah, made the feet of Judah, between which the law-giver came at the close of law given to Shem?

These are Barbarians, Romans, Saxons. Danes, Normans—a constitutional monarchy granting toleration under Elizabeth—a military theocratic despotism under the Puritan Cromwell. This last name is given for the want of a more appropriate one to convey the sense.

As in the case of Julian, the seventh head of Pagan Rome went back to the sixth; so it was in England, the seventh head under Cromwell went back to the sixth. The same is true in reference to Bonaparte. The seventh head went back to the sixth as the Bourbons. The seventh in each " continued for a short space." Louis Napolean stands now the eighth seventh revived head of West Rome, as Napolean Bonaparte was the seventh. We come now to the Israel of law in the land of Japheth's enlargement as the United States.

The seven heads of law are Spain, France, England. A scattered head, when sovereignty rested with the States. A united head, when the union was formed. A divided head at the Missouri Compromise, upon the doctrine of "States Rights." A head of forcible consolidation, upon both civil and moral questions as at present. Each side claimed forcible consideration. The one over the whole land, the other in its separate jurisdiction, by prohibiting any but slaveholding States into the Union. These seven heads apply alike to either side of the dividing line, and are thus twice counted as in the Israel from Shem. When the prophet says: "I will restore your judges as at first." It not only means they shall be chosen by the people, as in literal Israel, but it means there shall be the same in number to represent the twice seven counted heads. It means that there shall be seven out of one wing, and seven out of the other. The seven to represent the Southern wing are, Washington, Jefferson, Madison, Monroe, Jackson, Tyler, Polk. The seven to represent the other are, John Adams, J. Q. Adams, Van Buren, Harrison, Fillmore, Pierce, Buchanan. This does not include Zachary Taylor; the reason is given: Who Shiloh, as the head of the church, came out of the tribe of Judah, in national Judah, that was made up of both Benjamin and Judah, the scepter was to depart from nationa Judah. The ten kingdoms of West Rome are the ten tribes as Ephraim, The United States stood for both Benjam and Judah, in its undivided form. In their divided for the South is national Judah, and the North is Benjamin. Leah retook the husband from Rachel at the coming of the tribe of Zubulon or Florida, in 1821, that she might separate Benjamin and Judah in this land, which was done by the Missouri Compromise, set up that same year. Law was shown by the first settlement of Leah, which ended with the tribe of Judah, or Georgia—National Judah alone was required to point out both law and gospel.

David, as civil law, was put up at Philadelphia. This was David with seven wives. In order to find which one of the seven stood for the bride to David, or civil law, it was necessary for Leah to bring forth National Judah.

As the Shiloh, a head of the church, came of the tribe of Judah in the person of the Rev. James Andrew, in 1844–6, the time had come for the scepter to leave National Judah as the South. Law always closes with James. The Apostle James is law. Law had gone through this land in the length of it and breadth of it, "at the close of the last Southern or seventh judge, as James K. Polk. That which began with Washington, at the Atlantic Ocean, had landed at the Pacific Ocean. God had said, when Shiloh came, the scepter should depart. Gen. Taylor was elected out of Judah, contrary to the law of God, in 1848, hence he is not reckoned among the judges. Zachary Taylor fills three important characters in Israel. He is the Zachariah, the son of Jeroboam the second. He is Zachariah the prophet, slain between the temple and the altar. He is the prophet Zachariah, of whom Christ speaks as the first righteous blood that was shed. He stands as the first martyr to God's broken laws. We cannot enter here into a question of such deep interest. Forcible, Saul, as a civil law, had intruded upon David as the law of God. Rachel died at the birth of Benjamin, as Texas.

The Wilmot Proviso said to David, you shall have no

more territory. That which began with Abimilech as the seventh judge, agreeing with Andrew Jackson, the seventh in this land, had come to be a king of force for which Saul stood. The law for which Abraham stood as the first head of law, was changed into the first king by the will of man, and God called it Saul. This Saul came of national Benjamin; this Saul is the product of the seventh head of England, as the Puritan Cromwell, representing in this land the Plymouth colony. The other seventh head as Bonaparte of France, represents the Orleans territory. These two sevenths, standing for gospel given to Japheth in Europe, are the extremes of this Israel of law in the land of Japheth's enlargement. The one looked upon man as wholly a literal being or beast, and had the right to eat and drink, because "death was an eternal sleep." The other regarded him as wholly a supernatural being, and it was right to punish a man for kissing his wife on Sunday. If the one has no law but that of nature, the other allows no body to the law of God, but takes it all to be spiritual—neither of these are David; David has both a body and a soul — a civil and a church law. If for the church, he has a Joshua, and an Andrew, he has for the body a Jefferson and a Hambleton. If David has not his same soul or church at his second annointing, by national Judah, in Naphtali, as the place of Rachel's triumph, he has another Jefferson and Hambleton coming out of literal Judah, or "between his feet," to represent the body. Perhaps the reader will think we write enigmatically—then let him study to solve the enigma. All things are not expedient in this land of peace. "That determined upon shall be accomplished." The seven times seven heads of nations make forty nine, and God's jubilee has come, in which he means to vindicate his own laws for his creation—man. These seven nations are the seven pillows, which wisdom has hewn out, one out which to build her house, in order to the reign of Solomon. It was the earth " that helped the woman or Bible."

The trinity of heads as Spain, France, England, which stand as the trinity of Abraham, Isaac Jacob, or Saul, David. Soloman, to literal Israel, are as Moon, Sun, Earth. Spain is the world's literal Moon, France is the literal Sun. France attains the highest perfection in all things that the merely intellectual man can reach. Briton is guided more by the laws of God, and hence " the earth." The minature world " helped the woman." Out of Briton came the laws to make David. David was annointed as the eight son of Jessee ; David stood as the summary of the seven. The seven forms of government which England had, stand as the seven sons of Jessee. The prophet asked Jessee, when passing his sons under review, "Are these all thy sons." The answer was, "The youngest is with the sheep out in the wilderness."

England had passed through every form of government, both from without and within, but she had organized a different form from any of these for her colonies in the wilderness—this form consisted of "local charters. This was the form for David. The literal Israel were forbid to carry "the inheritance," or laws of one tribe into those of another. This was God's provision to settle Israel after her "old estates," and hence this was David. Each tribe in Israel had its local Elders, and then a Sanhedrim to represent the whole upon questions that pertained to all the tribes alike. The literal David came at the end of fourteen generations, from "Abraham to David."

The seven heads of Papal Rome, in the land of Japheth, and the seven of England, make fourteen, to the rise of David upon the form of "local charters." From David to the captivity were fourteen.

The seven presidents, or heads in this land, from the North, and the seven from the South, make fourteen, and Israel is in captivity. Fourteen are yet lacking, which must come in one cycle of Orion, or eighty-four years from 1860–1, which will give to each judge, or head, six years. Let this pass. Out of Briton, or the earth that combine both sun and moon, not only came David as the civil, but David as the soul law. As she sent the civil law of David away, differing from any law she had had, so she sent the soul law that stood for David, differing from anything she had had. These make Joseph, at whose birth it is said, "Send me away to my people and country." The church of John, the forerunner, was organized with a bishop for its head, yet not diocesian. This two was the seventh to agree with David. The seven churches, as wives of David, are the Puritan, of Massachusetts; the Baptist, of Rhode Island; the Dutch Reformed, of New York; the Quaker, of Pennsylvania; the Catholic, of Maryland; the church of England, as Virginia; the church of Wesley, dating from Georgia to Philadelphia. "Kings and their Queens not only had to be the nurses" of the "Restored Japhetic Israel," but the religion of the king or queen, was also to represent the religion of the tribe for which these stood. The mother-in-law, Naamah, which dates from church and State union, under Constantine, as "Tubalcain and his sister, Naamah," and which was the first form of the church after Cain or the Israel of law, was cast out, is the same as Naomi or Rome, and is represented by Catholic Mary, or

Catholic Maryland. The daughter that followed the mother as Ruth, is Elizabeth, or Virginia, (the virgin queen.) Orpha standing for all the Congregational churches, represents, the Puritan, of Massachusetts; the Baptist, of Rhode Island; the Dutch Reformed, of New York; the Quaker, of Pennsylvania. The head to represent these coming from England was Cromwell.

We are debtor to Rev. C. Elliot for saying George the III was a "Wesleyan Methodist," representing the tribe of Judah or Georgia, at which tribe Leah left bearing. Louisiana, bearing the name of Louis XIV, is the tribe to represent the religion of France, when pursuing the laws of nature, and burning the Bible, "the Sun became as black as sackcloth of hair."

Not only did "the earth," or England, help the women in showing how Israel would be settled according to the teachings of "the woman," but she was the chosen Egypt as the place of learning to overcome the confusion of Babylon. James is law. When her own King James gathered together all the teachings of the woman, and had them put into a book and translated into a "pure language," the confusion of Babel was overcome; nothing has been added since. God's symbols say (the book) was finished. There is no need to go back to Egypt or Babylon, to learn the truth. It is written in God's own Book, and God's history.

It is from the book that the truth is learned that Abraham moves as "the Father," Isaac as "the Son," and Jacob as "God the Holy Ghost." Men will never learn from Babylon the difference which God makes between Baal and Balak, and Balaam and Baalzebub, and Jerrubaal, nor will they learn the difference between Eli and Elijah, and Elisha, and Eliphaz, and Elihu, and Elizabeth and Elias. There are a number of things that cannot be learned from Babylon. Men must come to Jerusalem to learn—God will be the teacher. He is the only Rabbi. If England was less corrupted with the one language of mystical Babylon than any nation in the land of Japheth, or gospel Israel, it is because she was the farthest removed from the seat of Babylon. It is, perhaps, due to this fact that she was the first to throw off the yoke of Babylon. That she was God's chosen land to provide the great principles of laws to rule in the Japhetic Israel, is the demonstrative truth. It is her own Usher that has given the best chronology of the "woman" the world has had, because the nearest conformed to the demonstrative facts.

As Ham had to serve Japheth in the land of his enlargement, in accordance with the second covenant set with

Abraham, it is England's first protestant and greatest queen, that was used as an instrument to "help the woman," and she traded in the persons of Ham.

As the Israel from Shem had been trained in Egypt for the nationality in Canaan, so the Israel from Japheth with all the laws to govern it, came out of Egypt or Briton, as "the earth that helped the woman," Joshua, the first judge of the literal Israel came of Ephraim as the ten tribes; so George Washington, the first judge of the Japhetic Israel, stood as the embodiment of all that was good, or noble, or praiseworthy, that had been brought forth by the ten kingdoms of West Europe, as Ephraim.

The doctrines of Magna Charter, habeas corpus, toleration, or what not, met in him. He was ever distrustful of himself, yet was found equal to any task, whether great or small, laid upon him.

If the name of Joshua was changed from that of Oshua, the name of Washington was changed to that of "the father of his country," not to mention any other change. If Joshua implies the deliverer, the other was the deliver. If the first presided over thirteen tribes, counted as twelve, so did the other. If the first was seen all alone talking with a man with a drawn sword, and asked him, "Art thou for us or our enemies;" and he was commanded to "Loose the shoes from thy feet, for the ground upon which thou standest is holy;" " I am come as the captain of the Lord's hosts." The other was seen all alone, on bended knees, talking with God. If the first had no literal children, but had the care of all Israel, the same is true of the other.

If the law-giver (Moses) of the first did not enter the land of Canaan, but stood upon Nebo and looked over all the land, it was to represent the law-giver (Christ) of the second who is higher than Moses, and looks not only over all the land, but looks, and sees, and knows all things that every one is doing, whether openly or in secret, and who intends to find out every Achan in Israel before it is done. If Joshua in making his farewell address to Israel, tells them how God brought them "across the flood," and settled them in the land, it was the nation of the other, that in very truth had come " across the flood," as the Atlantic Ocean, and gave to the Japhetic Israel his dying charge. If the Israel of the first which came from Shem, had fourteen civil judges, and then two kings, as the representatives of human and divine laws, so the Israel of the second, given to Japheth, has had fourteen civil judges, and then two kings, as Saul and David, to represent the laws of God and the laws of man. If the Israel of the first extended over a space of many hundred years in setting the types to bring forth the laws of God, that met on "the Christ," the Israel of the second has done in eighty-four years, or in one day, or one cycle of Orion, what it required a month of cycles to do in the other. This month of cycles includes the whole of God's indignation against Israel, and is 2520 years. The last end of the indignation is 1260 years. The count begins with the center head of the forty-nine, as the "little horn" that come up among the ten horns, or kingdoms of West Rome, and that claimed both civil and soul laws, and in accordance with this claim placed the crown on Pepin of France. Three times and a half, are three and one-half of the seven nations, each with seven heads, and are forty-two months or 1260 years, or forty-two literal years, or if counted as an hour, are the twenty-fourth part of eighty-four years, or three years and a half, as the length of time for God's witnesses to be dead. If power was given into the hands of this horn, which claimed both departments of the kingdom in the years 606-8, then the church as one witness should stand upon its feet in 1866, and the civil in 1868. Let these thoughts pass for the present.

If the Israel of the first Joshua divided into two parts, between ten tribes and two tribes, not only that the two that stood for the laws of God, might bring forth "the Christ," but also that the ten might show how gospel Israel would act in the second half of Israel in the land of Japheth or Europe, so the Israel of the second Joshua has divided between ten tribes and four tribes, not only to show that the ten will act in accordance with the ten in the Israel of Shem, or in that of Japheth in Rome, while the four will not only bring forth the laws of God, but will show what have been the four forms under which the church has moved, and will stand as the four books of law given by Moses, or four books of gospel given by Christ, or as the world's four law-givers, or as the four first-born sons of Leah. These four are the four original tribes of this Israel, common to both the first and second settlement of Israel. That is, the Israel of law and the Israel of both law and gospel. Like as it required gospel Israel to explain that of law, so it requires this second settlement of Israel, in the land of Japheth to explain the first as law. The tribes of the first can only be understood as they hold relation to the second. If in the investigation we should use the word "Confederacy," it is out of no disrespect to God's prophet, which says, "Say ye not a confederacy, a confedracy, but sanctify the Lord of hosts and let him be your fear."

The four tribes or States, common to both settlements of

this Israel, are Virginia, North Carolina, South Carolina and Georgia. These are:
Virginia as Reuben.
North Carolina as Simeon.
South Carolina as Levi.
Georgia as Judah.

This is the manner in which they have been transferred out of Israel's past history. Of Levi came the law-giver, Moses; of Judah, came the law-giver, Christ. These are South Carolina and Georgia. The laws for which these stand are the two wings with which the cherubim covers his face. These are the only two of the first settlement of this Japhetic Israel, found among the seven in which Rachel triumphed as the "seven eyes of God." Among the seven that cut the stone (as the laws of God) out of the mountain, will be found the six wings of the cherubim, "with twain he covered his feet." This twain are Joseph and Benjamin, symbolically the very same as the two first. Joseph is the church and Benjamin is law; as a literal tribe, he is Texas. If the church came in 1844, Benjamin came in 1845. The twain with which he did fly are the twain with which God has moved. They are Moon and Sun; Spain and France, Florida and Louisiana. Florida came in 1821 as the law or moon. Forty years from this, in 1861, law prevailed in Naphtali. Louisiana came in 1803–4; forty years from this coming, and the gospel Sun came in 1844; the very same two that journeyed forty years from "the earth," as combining both moon and sun from Judah or Georgia, to Philadelphia, are the two of Rachel's triumph in Naphtali, both as a place and character. This she never could have done had she not conformed soul law to civil law. If Moses said, Canaan shall serve Japheth, the church had no right to say, "Slavery was a great evil." The literal Moses had an Ethiopian wife, so the bride to the law of Moses must be an Ethiopian bride, and recognize the law of Moses. When the church published her law, leaving out all condemnation of slaveholding in 1860–1, and conformed to Moses, Rachel triumphed. The witnesses might have put off their sackcloth, but for the seven years, as the summary of the seven times, to keep David out of his dominions according to the types. Half of which seven times Israel had to fight as law, and half to suffer as gospel.

The four States, common to the double settlement of this Israel, include the entire history of Israel. The law given by Levi or Moses, and for which the son of Rachel as Benjamin stood in its undivided form, became as Reuben, the first-born son of Leah, after it divided. It ceased to be

Benjamin after Israel divided; Benjamin is unity, Reuben is duality; the gospel given by Judah, standing for Joseph, the son of Rachel, became Simeon and Levi, when it united State and church in Rome. The law of this Japhetic Israel was Benjamin as unity, upon the doctrine of "State rights," and Ham, as a servant of tribute, according to Moses, when it was first formed. This was the teaching of both Reuben the first, as Virginia, and Simeon the second, or Plymouth colony. If these rejected the word (slavery) from the law, and softened it down by the term "domestic institutions," it was still recognized as the law, by the rendition of the slave escaping from one tribe into another. This law also said "Governments were by consent of the governed." The laws of God for this Israel of Shem were contradictory. If the one said, "Thou shalt not kill;" the other said, "Without the shedding of blood is no remission." This contradiction is intentional upon the part of God to show that he is the only king. The laws of this Japhetic Israel are also contradictory. The doctrine of "State rights" is the law of Moses or David, or Benjamin. The doctrine that "Governments are by consent of the governed," brought forth Saul the first king in the Israel of Shem. Tribes cannot be forbidden to carry the inheritance or laws of one into another, and then turn and say, "Governments are by consent of the governed." In every case it will result as in both the Israel from Shem, and that of Japheth. God cannot be the king of two such contradictory laws, only for a demonstrative purpose. If the law had read, governments are by the consent of the sons of Japheth, when taken in their tribe or State capacity, it would have been the truth, as will be seen by the teachings of the children of Rachel in this demonstrative Israel. God will add all the plagues of his book to men until they cease to mend it. The law of unity, for which Benjamin stood in this Israel, was driven out when the tribe of Benjamin was driven out. This was done by both Reuben and Simeon, in the persons of James Monroe and J. Q. Adams, when they sold Benjamin, or Texas, for Florida, in 1821. Florida is Zebulon. This tribe was not consulted in reference to whether he would unite with Israel. It was a law of force and all intentional upon the part of God to make the Israel that should teach both law and gospel. If Reuben stands for the two tribes, as under RChoboam that were to bring the Christ, Simeon stands for the ten that built "golden heifers" under Jeroboam; if Reuben represents the ceremonial law, Simeon, standing for all the churches holding to Presbyterian ordination as Levi, and uniting with Simeon in this land to worship a great image, the same as Simeon and Levi united in Rome. The gospel which came from Judah, as in Christ, became united with Simeon in Rome, and became very cruel. So the gospel that dates from Judah in this land, headed by Wesley and put up at Philadelphia has become united to Simeon in this land, and has become very cruel. This is the way God leads Israel to show that he is king, and that God and the laws, or word of God, are one. The mending of the word of God is the mending of God, or the making of another God.

Simeon is God's hostage to drive Israel to take Benjamin; Simeon in Rome killed the martyrs as God's witnesses; Simeon as "the Spanish Jesuit," drove God's Israel to the nationality in this land. Simeon, as Plymouth, has again driven Israel to show both law and gospel. Religion is no more free than "governments are by consent." If God says, "Ye must be born again," he means what he says: Men may for a while climb up some other way, yet the book cannot be mended. If God says, Paul was the head of all the churches; God will have a head according to his own teaching. Not as an office only, but also as an order, to which we will come after awhile. "Simeon and Levi shall be scattered in Israel." It is to this demonstrative Israel these servants are transferred to fill up this part of their history. Taken in this land, to scatter Simeon and Levi, they are North and South Carolina. If these four tribes be applied to Israel's history, in connection with the four books of law as given by Moses, Reuben is the Exodus, and stands for the beginning of Israel in Egypt. Simeon is the Book of Numbers and stands for the second Israel in the land of Japheth or Rome, when the God of forces or numbers was the God of men. Levi is Leviticus to represent the church both with Reuben and Simeon. Judah is Duteroniny, which closes the settlement of Israel and gives the symbolic history for which they stand. As this is done in this land, it closes the law and "finishes the mystery." The same facts apply to the four books of the evangalists. Mark and Luke are only servants to Mathew and John.

Jacob is God the Holy Ghost. Two of his wives are only given as servants of the other two. If Leah is Reuben, Rachel is Judah. These are "the first and the last." Reuben as Virginia, is the first; Judah as Georgia, is the last. If Reuben is law as "State rights," he is not gospel as "Freedom in religion. The law-givers out of Judah or from between his feet, as Jefferson Davis and A. H. Stevens, hold the same law of Reuben, as "States rights," while Andrew out of Judah is given to show not "freedom in religion," but ye must be born again. "Judah is my law-giver." If Reuben defiled himself by the ordinance of 1787, saying, Ham should not be a servant, then God makes James Andrew of Judah, a slaveholder. As Eve had led Adam astray, "the seed of the woman or church should triumph," and bring that Adam back to the laws of God. It is the civil law for which Adam stands, that the church is to bring back. As the church has led the world away from the law of Moses, so the church shall bring it back to that law. This is the simple sense.

We have traced the history of Israel from Adam through Cain down to the political organization of the Japhetic Israel as Lamech at Philadelphia. The church has been considered from Eve down through the line of Seth to Lamech, and put up at Philadelphia. It has been seen that the Meshich from Shem, and the Meshech from Japheth, meet in the land of North America, when Japheth is "enlarged over Shem. All that was left of the Israel of Shem was the "woman that had the moon under her feet and a crown of twelve stars upon her head." This woman is the word of God. She was hid in the convents of the Romish Monks till the "breaking of the day" at the reformation. She was helped by Briton, as the minature world that gave shape and form to the woman. Out o' her seventh head as Cromwell, and her sixth as Elizabeth, which two are Ruth and Orpha, between these as the feet of Judah or gospel, came John Wesley; so between the seventh head as Cromwell, and the seventh of Rome as Bonaparte, came the Israel of law in the twelve tribes of the gospel Israel given to Japheth in the land of his enlargement over Shem. These laws make David as the civil law, yet it was David with seven wives. One wife to represent each of the seven heads of law in England, according to all the former types.

This Israel of Lamech had a double work to do in slaying an old man, as "the divine right of one man to rule upon the doctrine that governments are by consent;" and also, a young man that says, "All men have the right to rule, and religion must conform to this declaration of the natural man. Neither of these are the laws of God as "husband and bride," and hence Lamech must slay them both. If with the Israel of law he slayed the first as one man, it is with the Israel of both law and gospel, he will slay the second.

The work on hand is to settle the second Israel, and tell that distinct character or thing, for which each of the twelve tribes stand. The woman has brought forth the man-child to represent the laws of God, and the dragon stands ready to devour him as soon as he is born. The tail of the dragon has drawn a third part of the moon, or Israel of law, which was made up of twelve tribes. Four is the third part; and a third part of the stars or States, as gospel. These are the third part, whether counted as ten or as eleven, as there were thirty-three States at the division of the gospel church, or whether as twelve or the third part of thirty-six as at present. The dragon says these shall follow his lead. This dragon is the "Nahash" that was begotten by Adam and Eve, in the first test act of God with man. In the second test act, he was shown in the natural man Ham. He was again presented in Esau. In the seventh head of Papal Rome, he was presented in the form of the "French infidelity." In this land, he is called "the dragon;" his right name is Haman or Ham-man, or the national man in contrast with the laws of God as set in Abraham.

It is an act of sovereignty with God to make one party represent his laws as written, and another the law of the "Nahash" or natural man. This is the way he moves to represent his laws and human laws. As the Israel of law given to Shem, united with the eagle of Pagan Rome to kill "the Christ" or man-child, so the eagle of America, as the Israel of law given to Japheth, has left the law and killed the nation to take the law as the man-child which "the woman" has brought forth. God has said it should go just that way. God hath put it into the hearts of the ten horns, or ten toes, or ten tribes, called horns, because they are the opposite of the ten commandments of Moses, or Benjamin, "to give their power and strength to the beast," or Nahash or dragon, until they should compel Israel to demonstrate the laws of God.

Let us apply the image of Nebuchadnizzard as interpreted by Daniel, to the history of Israel, as it extends to the three grand divisions of Israel, as Asia, Europe and America. "The head of gold" is Babylon; the arms of silver is "the medo-Persian kingdom;" the thighs of brass," the Macedonian or Grecian kingdom; the legs of iron, the Roman kingdom, or Pagan Rome. The ten horns that mixed "iron and clay," the ten kingdoms of West Rome that united State and church: "the mountain," the United States, "the stone cut out of the mountain without hands," the seven States that first organized the Southern Confederacy. These seven are no accidental seven. They are the only seven in the land that could represent the twice counted seven heads of the land. These were cut out "without hands" to fill the types for which they stood. Spain, the first head, is Florida; France, is Louisiana; these are moon and sun—England as "the earth," is Georgia. As law and gospel count forty years from the two first for the second settlement of Israel, so law and gospel both count from the tribe of Judah or Georgia, to represent "the earth" forty years to Philadelphia, for the first settlement. South Carolina, separated from North Carolina, stands for the scattered head, the same as Jacob's family was scattered by the sale of Joseph. Benjamin is law, to represent Texas as "the united head." The divided head is the literal division between the two tribes of Judah, as Alabama and Mississippi. These were one, and were divided as Israel divides, and stand as the sixth or divided head. The four other States as Virginia, North Carolina, Tennessee and Arkansas, that came voluntarily to the seven, make the seventh head of choice. These are no accidental four, as will be seen before we are done.

While this prophecy of Daniel applies in its extended sense to the whole history of Israel, it also applies to either wing of Israel—whether to literal Israel as the type given to Shem, or to gospel Israel given to Japheth in Rome, or to the Israel in the land in which Japheth is "enlarged over Shem." What now is the predicate of this prophecy in the Israel of law given to Shem? In the days of its unity, it was the "Head of gold." Its duality make the the "Arms of silver." The ten tribes are the "Brass," and also the ten that mixed "Iron and Clay." The two tribes, as Benjamin and Judah, are the "Legs of iron," because they stand for the laws of God, that are to "stamp the whole earth," symbolized by Rome that claimed the world. "The mountain" was the land of Shem, or Israel, in the land of Shem. The stone was "the Christ" which was brought forth, or the laws of God, as written in his book. These are one and the same. The Son of God and the word of God are one. The reflective mind can apply the facts to the Israel of Japheth as Europe. Let them be applied to the Israel of North America. In the days of Israel's unity, it was "the head of gold; when it divided by the Missouri Compromise it was the "Arms of silver." The ten tribes of the North, as the ten original States are both the "brass" kingdoms. and also the ten that "mix iron and clay." "The legs of iron" are the laws of God that retire to the South. "The mountain" is the whole land, and the "stone cut out it," are the seven States that first withdrew from the mountain to show to the world what are the laws of God as written in his word. These are simply Moses and Christ, or they are David.

The cutting out of this stone began with Levi or South Carolina as the tribe of God's selection to bring Israel to the law of God. This Levi stood alone in this Japhetic Israel to bring Israel back to Moses, the same as in the Israel of Shem. Let this pass for the present until the tribes are settled and that distinct thing for which each one stands is pointed out.

Should any tribe complain of that part it has to act in the demonstration, let such tribe remember it is the God of Heaven that is using these tribes to show that he rules in the affairs of men, and that he rules by his own laws; and to complain would be to act as Cain, and that God would say to such tribe "Sin lieth at the door."

We come now to settle Israel, and tell what principle of law for which each tribe stands according to the prophecies of Moses and Jacob who as "God the Holy Ghost" in blessing the tribes, said, "I will tell you what will befall you in the last days," or for what you will stand in the last days of the Japhetic Israel of both law and gospel; as if he had said, these twelve sons are chosen as the representatives of God's laws for his creature man. These laws are his two witnesses, when they have finished their testimony, and the time comes for them to put off their "sackcloth and ashes," it will be because a nation has been brought forth as a land in which the tribes will be given to show that symbolic sense in which you, as the heads of Israel, have been used. This will be required to overcome that "Nahash," begotten by Adam and Eve, as the natural inclination of man to disregard the laws of the Creator. As God has used the sons of Adam, Cain, Abel, Seth, to represent his laws, so has he used the "Nahash," begotten by the disobedience of Adam and Eve, as his servant to drive Isaac to fulfill his will. The inclination to follow the beast, or nature, is God's whip of cords that puts his witnesses in sackcloth. As these witnesses have come through reproach, and God intends they shall be the king, they will stand to fulfill the prophecy of Pilate, when he said, "What I have written I have written." The king of the Jews. Ah! the king of the world.

Sincerely do we wish that the reader undertood the names of these tribes by the names that Jacob gave them.

It would save an amount of labor in the double repetition that is required to keep up the connected sense, to the mind which has not learned how to use the one for the other.

The four first-born sons of Leah are: Reuben is Virginia, Simeon is North Carolina, Levi is South Carolina, Judah is Georgia.

The two of Rachel's maid servant: Dan is Tennessee. Naphtali is Alabama.

The two of Leah's maid servant: Gad is Arkansas. Asher is Mississippi.

The two of Leah's when she began to bear again. Issachar is Louisiana, Zebulon is Florida.

The two of Rachel as Benjamin and Joseph. To Joseph the birthright was given, and he is both sun and moon, or civil and soul laws. Benjamin is Texas.

Joseph is the civil government put up by the seven in Naphtali, and "the Methodist Episcopal church, South." The two half tribes of Joseph as Manassah and Ephraim, are half tribes because they divine the man between soul and body, or civil law and soul law. These came with the church in its division yet in the civil division they came not. These are: Manassah as Kentucky, Ephraim is Missouri.

These are enough for God's demonstration. No human ingenuity can add one to the number. Nor can one be made to take the place of another. Come here, all of you, belonging to earth's great ones; come here, and let us see how God himself talks with his creature man. Don't be ashamed to come because it is an humble, obscure, unlearned, slaveholding *farmer* (that was) invites you. The author never went anywhere, and never saw anything; to use a phrase of easy comprehension, he is nobody; you never heard of him, and he hopes you never will. The writer is too simple to do anything further than to follow God's types as he gave them, and God's history as he fulfills them. Let the theologian lay aside his commentaries and come to the Book of God. God has told you no man "in heaven nor in earth could unloose the seals and open the book;" He has told us at the sounding of the seventh trumpet, or at the rise of the seventh nation, each with seven heads. When he shall begin to sound, the first thing announced is, "the mystery of God is finished;" man could not finish it, but God has. God has told us that "fire should go out of the mouth of his two witnesses and burn up their enemies." Then come here and let us see how God talks. Let the lawyer lay aside his books, the doctor his physic, the merchant his merchandise, the man of fiction his "yellow covers," the mechanic his tools, the farmer his plow, and let all classes come here. No matter about the obscurity or humility of the pilot; we will take the shortest cut, and promise not to detain you long. We will touch lightly, and leave each one to find out wonders of which they have not dreamed. You must pause at every period until you get the sense; it is no trifling matter in which we are engaged. The land is full of prophets, and a noble band they make, all striving to peer into the ways of God with man. We love them every one for their efforts in the cause of truth. It may be a "Balwin," or a

"Baxter," or a "Waller," or a "Cox," or a "Cross," or a "Seat," or an "Ariel," or his reviewers, and many others. Gross darkness still covers the land. Come here my brother-laborers in the cause of God. We find no fault with any of you. We are no reviewer; yet in the language of Elihu to Job, "Suffer me a little and I will fetch my knowledge from afar, and ascribe righteousness to my maker. God's winnowing time has come; he means to weigh the world in an even balance. Himself will make the distinction between his own written laws, and the laws of the "Nahash," a natural man called "the beast." From the beginning he foreordained and decreed his own laws to govern his creature man in both soul and body. In reference to the future life, Christ died for all men, and he means to save those in Israel whom Rebecca (the church) can persuade to put on the right garment. Isaac's eyes are holden; Isaac, as the Christ, loved every "Hairy Esau." The light of nature is the law of God in heathen lands in contrast with the law of nature; the light of nature teaches the heathen world, "Thou shalt not kill;" "Thou shalt not steal." The law of nature contradicts these laws of God. The light of nature harmonizes in all things with the law of God. Those who have not the written law will be judged by the light of nature in contrast with the law of nature. God is not a hard master; He does not reap where he does not sow; it was an act of sovereignty with God to select the seed of Abraham, with which to demonstrate his laws. The literal descent of the literal Israel given to Shem was not more literal and restricted to a certain line from Abraham through Isaac, and Jacob, and Joseph, and the two sons of Joseph, than has the line of gospel descent given to Japheth, been through the same line. Room was found for Israel in the two sons of Joseph, Manassah and Ephraim; these are law as Manassah, and law and gospel in Ephraim. These as literal tribes in this land are Kentucky and Missouri. These as two cherubims make the flock of Joseph; Joseph as the laws of God "dwells between the cherubims;" these are the "tree of life that grows upon either bank of the river, whose leaves are for the healing of the nations."

This literal land is a talking prophet; every tribe in this Israel is a prophet; this is the family of Jacob. When this family left the house of Laban because " there remained no further inheritance for the wives of Jacob in their fathers house;" Laban pursued Jacob and laid claim to everything Jacob had. God appeared to Laban and told him to let Jacob alone. (We give the sense.) They formed a league and drew a line, and took an oath that neither should cross that line for harm to the other. Jacob erected a pillow and called it Galeed or Gilead, in token of the covenant made; Mt. Ephraim was in the land of Gilead. In this Israel Ephraim is Missouri, and that line is called the Missouri Compromise line. Did God approve of this line? In the same sense in which he has approved of the whole history of Israel, he did. This is what we call a demonstrative sense. In order to select the tribes to give the meaning to his laws, it was approved; as restricting the laws in their action to any boundary less than the world when the sense is finished, it has no authority in the word of God. "The stone out of the mountain must fill the world." If national Judah could have maintained that boundary made by the Missouri Compromise, he would have restricted the laws of God with which Abra-Ham is to possess the world within himself. The laws of God hold no compromise with the laws of men; the one is indulged on account of human weakness, and God uses it as an instrument to create strife to drive Israel to fulfill his word. God is opposed to a kingly government, yet he has granted it; God is opposed to a plurality of wives; yet he has granted it; God is opposed to Ham running at large as a beast, yet made in the image of God, yet he has granted it; God is opposed to Ham's ruling Japheth, and yet he grants it. None of these permits for demonstrative purposes will be allowed when the "mystery is finished," the times numbered, and the witnesses stand upon their feet. Things are permitted under "solemn protest." This is true in the Japhetic Israel, the same as that of Shem.

In the settlement of this Japhetic Israel of law, Reuben, or Virginia, was the first-born tribe, and Judah, or Georgia, was the last. In the settlement of the Israel of both law and gospel, the half tribe of Joseph, as Manassah, or Kentucky, was the first-born, and the tribe of Benjamin, as the tribe at which Rachel died is the last. This tribe is Texas. The mess of Benjamin was five times as large as any other mess. The literal fact will in every respect be found to agree with the prophetic fact. This tribe of Benjamin is five times as large as any other tribe.

The literal Joseph, like Jacob, or Abraham, standing for the laws of God, set each one's mess to itself, thereby showing each tribe would stand to itself. To each tribe Joseph gave one change of raiment to set forth the double type of laws for which they stood. To the tribe of Benjamin he gave "five changes of raiment." This was done to show the five different things for which Benjamin stood. These five things for which Benjamin stands in the history of

Israel, are the following: First—he is the law of Moses written in ten commandments; secondly—he is the Israel of law given to Shem, to whom the law was given; thirdly, he is the law of the nation given to the Japhetic Israel, in the land of Japheth's enlargement, when the union was first formed; fourthly—he is the nation that first formed the law upon the doctrine of "local charters" or "States rights;" fifthly—as a tribe in Israel, he is "the Lone Star, Texas." As the literal Israel from Shem moves in the world with the law of Moses, for which they stand as the body, or civil law of of the body, so does the tribe of Benjamin in this Japhetic Israel move with the law for which he stands.

It was Reuben, the first-born son of Jacob, that stood pledged to bring Benjamin. This Reuben must do in the five different characters for which Benjamin stands. Reuben said, "If I bring not Benjamin, slay my two sons." Reuben is Virginia. The two sons of this Reuben are "States Rights and Freedom in Religion." It was the doubting Thomas, standing as the dividing apostle to represent the second half, who is in this land represented by the doubting Thomas Jefferson as the second Southern judge in this Israel, that bought the second half of this Israel in the Louisiana purchase, in which the tribe of Benjamin is included. This was done by this son of Reuben in 1803–4, as the years of purchase and exchange of treaties. This act was approved because Rachel then held the husband, as the civil government in the stead of Leah. As the literal Israel, as Benjamin, was cast out by the joint action of Reuben and Simeon, upon the division of Israel between law and gospel, so did Reuben and Simeon in this land cast out the tribe of Benjamin, or Texas, and also the law of Benjamin upon a division of this Japhetic Israel by the Missouri Compromise of 1821. Reuben as Virginia, and Simeon as Plymouth, in the persons of J. Monroe and J. Q. Adams, gave Benjamin, or Texas, in exchange for Zebulon, or Florida, in the year 1821, and gave the husband to Leah by the act, and cast out both the law of Benjamin that united Israel, and the tribe of Benjamin that moves with the law. This act was done to separate ten tribes from the two. It was intentional on the part of God in order to show what were the civil law, and soul law, for which the two tribes stood. The representatives of these laws, as collective bodies, had to be gathered alone in national Judah. That Reuben, that first brought Benjamin to represent the whole of this Israel of law, in the person of Thomas Jefferson, and which cast Benjamin out in the person of James Monroe, still stood pledged to bring Benjamin back. It was only for a time

Benjamin was to be cast out. The same is true in reference to the law of Moses, as Benjamin, or the Jews as Benjamin, or the nation of Benjamin, in the land of Japheth's enlargement. If Reuben and Simeon, in this land, in casting out Benjamin, acted the kingly parts of the first and second Israel's, as in Judah and Rome. In bringing Benjamin back, Reuben and Levi acted the parts for which they stood in this restored Japhetic Israel; if force cast out Benjamin, the principle of choice brought him back. The representative heads to do this were, John Tyler, of Reuben, and John Calhoun of Levi. As the literal Reuben put Joseph, who stands for God's dual laws, in the pit, intending to take him away, so Reuben in this land put Benjamin in the pit, which Benjamin stands for the one-half, or civil law of Joseph in the pit, with the intention of taking him away. It was only "for the present," as said James Monroe, of Reuben, that the act was done. "For the present we ought to be content with the Floridas." Reuben could not have brought Benjamin back upon the principles of God's laws to govern Israel by choice, and not force; had not God removed Gen. Harrison, in order to place a son of Reuben at the head of the nation, this son of Reuben was John Tyler, who signed the bill to bring back Benjamin in the year 1845, three days before his term of office expired.

In the Israel of Shem, nine tribes and a half were located on the West of the Jordan, and two tribes and a half on the East. In the Israel of Japheth, nine tribes and a half are on the East of the Jordan, and two tribes and a half are on the West.

The two tribes and a half in Shem were Reuben the first born of Jacob, and Manassah the first-born of Joseph, and Gad the dividing tribe. In this Japhetic Israel, the first is last, and the last is first. The place of Reuben, the first-born of Jacob, is filled by Benjamin, the last born. The place of Manassah, the first-born of Joseph, is taken by Ephriam his younger brother, while Gad, the dividing tribe, holds his same position. Jacob crossed his hands willingly "in blessing the children of Joseph, to show the nature of this change in the anti-type given to Japheth. There are no mistakes in God's Book. All others that do not tend to explain this one, are of men, and they are of no use. Art, science, history, discovery, are God's exponents. If six tribes bless and six tribes curse, the meaning is, the one half of Israel is God's driving force, and the other half is the pulling force. The two tribes are symbolically the same as the ten. The two "golden heifers" of Jeroboam were the Gods of men, and stood as the substitutes of the two tribes, "Benjamin and Judah," as the representatives of the laws of God. The same truth applies to gospel Israel given to Judah in the land of Japheth in Europe. The ten kingdoms of West Rome, called "ten horns," stood to represent God's dual laws that were written in his Book, while these were hid in the convents of the Romish monks. The same fact applies to this restored Japhetic Israel. The ten old States in the North stand ,for the ten horns, or ten toes, that take the place of God's laws, or God's two witnesses, in this land. These claim to legislate for both departments of God's kingdom, and thus they do what God only claims the right to do. These ten are New Hampshire, Massachusetts, Rhode Island, Connecticut, Vermont, New York, New Jersey, Pennsylvania, Delaware, Maryland. These are the representatives of the west wing of Jeroboam, to represent ten tribes that substituted golden gods for the laws of God. These would not fill the former types, if they did not think they were doing right in their action. Truth is always in the rear with man. Man does not know the meaning God attaches to his own word, till in the pursuit of the laws of nature God points it out. The two kings, upon which the literal Israel divided as Rehoboam and Jeroboam were both born at Jerusalem. These were only a different form of presenting Saul and David. Manassah is the tribe to represent law as the son of Joseph, the same as Benjamin does Jacob. This tribe in this land is Kentucky; in this tribe was born Abraham Lincoln and Jefferson Davis. The law for which Abraham stood was changed at the seventh head, and forcible Saul came as the first king. The seventh President from the North in this land was James Buchanan. As James Polk closed the seven from the South, James Buchanan closed the seven from the North.

God commanded Saul in the battle with the Amelekites to take the lives of everything and take none of the spoils. God's prophet came to Saul and told him he had disobeyed God, that he heard the lowing of cattle and the bleating of sheep. Saul told the prophet that he had found out a better way of serving God than by following his directions. That in place of taking the lives of the sheep and cattle he intended them for sacrifice to the Lord. The prophet might have replied in substance to Saul: Of your sincerity in this matter there can be no doubt, but it has cost you your kingdom; God did not give you a law to mend, but a law to keep. The same facts apply to Uzzah who caught the ark when the oxen stumbled. God had said, none but the Levites should touch the ark. This was the law and stood paramount to any other consideration. If the Levites could not keep the ark from falling, then let it fall. The modern world seem to think it has a different God from the one who wrote his book. It is the world's mistake. If Saul thinks to mend God's law that says, "Ham, the father of Canaan, shall serve Japheth," and "Thou shalt not covet thy neighbors servant," Saul will find out his mistake after he has tried it. In worshipping Ham, the natural man, and not the law set in Abra-Ham, he may build his gallows fifty cubits high. This Ham-an will get upon his own gallows, and learn that God will have no amendments before it is done.

Turning now to the tribes of this Japhetic Israel. How can it be known of what God approves, and of what he disapproves? This settlement is made by "God the Holy Ghost," combining both the "Father and the Son," and moves with the literal acts of the literal Jacob.

The two wives of Jacob, as Rachel and Leah, are given to show of what God approves, and what not. All the children of Rachel are approved because the law ruling at the time of the birth of such tribe stands as the law of God. Those of Leah are not approved, because the church law for which she stands mixes human laws with the laws of God. The husband to Rachel is the law of Moses; the husband to Leah is the civil government reigning at the time the tribe is born. Once only is Jacob as "God the Holy Ghost," the husband of Leah, at the birth of her six children. This is at the birth of the tribe of Icsachar, the first tribe begotten with a bargain and sale, and he is given to represent the merchandise of Ethiopia and is made a servant of tribute. Leah changes the husband with every change of the civil government; Rachel's husband is unchangeable, and she dies when the husband is entirely taken from her. The seven years service of Jacob for Rachel is the seven years of war had in this Israel as the Israel of law. Jacob served for Rachel as the laws of God, but when the morning came, or the light broke, he found he had Leah. It is a prophecy in action, and he had both Leah and Rachel.

The church has been none the less the church of God because it has been struggling with the heathen laws of man, represented by Leah. Rachel is given to show what it will be when it comes to the laws of God, and ceases to cover itself with "fig-leaves." Leah adapts herself to every form of civil law under which the church has moved. Rachel has no king but the laws of God; Leah has kings, popes, and all of nature's "high nobility," for her husband. Rachel is unity upon God's laws for husband and bride; Leah is unity upon the laws of man for husband and bride. Leah divides

Israel; Rachel knows no division—the world is her parish; Leah is yielding to the caprices of human laws; Rachel will die before she will yield one hair's breadth; Leah is slaveholding at one time, and anti-slavery at another. Rachel says all the time, "Ham is a servant of tribute." The children of Leah will pass away after the demonstration is ended; the children of Rachel are perpetual and will live through the thousand years of rest to Israel. If in the settlement of this Israel of law with twelve tribes, in the land of Japheth's enlargement; Leah, as the mother. representing the four sons common to both settlements, she is Ruth, or Elizabeth. or the Church of England. Rachel stands for the one that was put up at the literal Philadelphia, after the forty years journeying in the wilderness from the tribe of Judah. This one is headed by George III, or John Wesley. If Leah stands for the seven scattered churches in the land, as the seven wives of David, Rachel is the Bath-sheba among the seven. If these seven, as the seven daughters of Reuel, are represented by Leah, Rachel is the Zepporah among the seven, with not the literal Moses, but with the law of Moses, for the husband. The contest in this Israel is narrowed down to the two wings of that single church put up at Philadelphia, at the head of whom stood John the "forerunner," as John Wesley. This was the one of whom it was said, "I will open a door to thee that no man will shut, and I will keep thee, and I will make the world come and worship at thy feet, and they shall know that I have loved thee." The death of all the other six is told. Even the one at Smyrna, as the Baptist church, designated by the two literal wives that followed David into the South land in the rebellion of Saul and Absalam against David, the death of this one, though highly commended, is told. The two churches that divided into this land, before this war, were the one at Smyrna, or Baptist church, and the one at Philadelphia, or Methodist church. Of the church at Smyrna, or the Baptist church, which stands to represent the congregational churches, it is said, "Thou art poor, yet making many rich; thou shalt not suffer persecution ten days, (or ten centuries) be thou faithful unto death and I will give thee a crown of life." While she teaches for the soul, "Ye must be born again." The church of God has a head. To Paul was committed the care of all the churches.

Again, we repeat, the contest is narrowed down to the two wings of the church of John Wesley, as first organized in this land at Philadelphia. Let us track God's types and see how the Holy Ghost moves to fulfill them in this demonstrative Israel. We say demonstrative Israel, because the whole, whether in church or State, is coming together again, and "Ephraim as the North, and Judah as the South, are going to appoint them one head," and that head will be God's written laws, and peace shall dwell between them. This will be after these have learned there can be no peace upon human laws or man's wisdom. History is ours. Things future belong to God, and we will try to avoid speculations as much as possible.

The verbs love, hate, joined, praise, judged, prevailed. dwell, &c., used by the mother at the birth of each child are given to show the relation which the child, or tribe, holds to the civil law, as the husband with the mother, representing the soul, or church of the soul. At the birth of the four first tribes, Leah is the mother and stands as the church of England, and the husband is the civil government of England, as these tribes were English colonies. They are also given to show how the divisions and laws governing Israel have been regarded by God in its past history, of which we cannot speak in this summary of Israel's history. Present facts are all aimed at.

At the birth of Reuben, (Virginia) Leah said, "Now will my husband love me." "Love me," stands for the child born. Did England, as the husband, love Virginia. The love for the parties was mutual, as is affirmed by all history. Turn to the next tribe as Simeon, or North Carolina. At the birth of this tribe, Leah said, "The Lord saw I was hated." What are the facts of history? This tribe was hated by England and she hated England as much as Virginia loved and was loved. If the one, as Virginia, offered an asylum to the deposed king, the other could hardly be made to submit to any governor the king would appoint. These tribes in this demonstrative Israel, hold that relation as the first and second that was held by the first Israel given to Shem, and the second given to Japheth. Let the question be understood. Seven years are in this land appointed for Jacob to get Rachel, that is to separate Rachel from Leah. As much is to be done in this seven years as during the whole seven times in the past history of Israel. The seven nations, each with seven heads, are seven times, and stand for the seven times that passed over Nebuchadnezzar in which he "ate grass like an ox," or followed the law of the beast, or law of nature. These seven times are seven years, at the close of which seven years, the entire history of the seven years is repeated. There is no incident in all of Israel's former history, that will not find its correspondent in this summary. Whether this be "the plagues of Egypt, or the ten persecutions, or the putting of the feet of Joseph in fetters; "they put his feet in fetters," or Daniel in the den of lions, the pursuit of Pharaoh, the captivity of Babylon, the delivery from Babylon, the re-building the temple, the coming of Christ, the stone placed upon him, the Roman guard to keep him from rising, the twelve patriarchs, or the twelve apostles. No matter what it may be, it will find its corresponding part, and its corresponding character, in this seven years war that is to show to the world both the husband and the bride.

These seven years are the "jubilee," to the seven times seven that have gone before. They stand as the seventh day to Joshua when he compassed Jerico. As much was done on the seventh day as had been done on all the other days; that is, they moved with rapid succession over the whole history of that which had gone before. All the heads, and law-givers, and kings, that Israel has ever had are herewith, the proper representatives that have come all the way down from Adam and Eve. It is the keeping these up in their symbolic character, that teaches what is civil law and church law. Not only what the laws are, but who compose those collective bodies to hold the laws.

At the birth of the third son, Leah said, "Now will my husband be joined to me." This tribe of Levi is South Carolina. It is a fact of history that in the year 1706, the civil law of England did establish the church of England in South Carolina. The establishing of the church in Reuben, or Virginia, was done by Sir Walter Raleigh, at its discovery, in the name of the Queen of England. This was not the method in which the husband was joined to the church in South Carolina. Levi was the tribe chosen to represent the ceremonial law of Moses, for which Leah stood in the Israel of Shem, when the Levites had no inheritance; Levi stood for Leah with the Pope of Rome, when Simeon and Levi "dug down a wall" and united State and church; Levi stood for Episcopal Ruth in England, and was Leah joined to her husband; Levi stood for the seven scattered churches in this land of Israel, when, as the Israel of law, these tribes had a common civil head, and Levi was "scattered in Israel," according to the declaration of Jacob, as " God the Holy Ghost." This Levi had no inheritance, as in the Israel of Shem. This Levi, standing for all the scattered churches, has again become united with Simeon, as in Rome, and Levi has an inheritance and the "birthright" is given to Joseph, who has no inheritance but a "double portion." None now belonging to Levi can pray only as Simeon dictates; Simeon standing as the "God of forces," or numbers, will not allow Levi to pray to a God that says, "Servants be obedient to your masters;" "Thou shalt not covet thy neighbors ox, nor servant." This Simeon knows no such God as this, and hence Levi, as Leah, is "joined to the husband." When this husband, as the civil, comes to the husband of Rachel, as the law of Moses, it is no longer Leah, but Rachel. We are not left to conjecture in reference to who stands as the civil judges of this Israel to represent both the husband and the bride.

At the birth of Judah, Leah said, "Now will I praise the Lord," "and Leah left bearing." Judah in this Israel stands as the fourth son of the second settlement of Israel, and is also the last of the first settlement. This tribe is Georgia. The whole settlement of this Japhetic Israel of law was Leah's, both in its civil department, with twelve patriarchs, and its church department, as seven churches. As Reuben the first and Judah the last were Leah's, with Levi standing for all the churches, so the whole included, between the first and last, were Leah's. The two sons of Rachel, as Joseph and Benjamin, stand for the heads of laws, and they do not come forth till after the forty years for Israel to "Journey in the Wilderness." As the tribe of Judah gave the world a Christ upon whom the laws of God met, in the Israel of Shem, so in the Israel of Japheth, these laws must take their rise from the tribe of Judah, each forty years to the place of union at Philadelphia. The birthright is given to Joseph, but Judah is the law-giver; that is, those dual laws of God, for which Joseph stands as the son of Rachel, and of which he is the type, must bring their heads for both civil and church, out of Judah.

The literal is given at every point, as the exponent of the symbolic. Four tribes, or four mothers, claimed all the territory belonging to the first Israel, not included in the domains of the other tribes. Reuben, as the first, claimed all the northwest; Simeon, the second, as Plymouth of the North, claimed Maine ; Simeon, of the South, as the second of the South, claimed Tennessee; Judah claimed all west of him to the Jordan or Mississippi river, as Alabama and Mississippi. There is no mistake, no merely happening in this arrangement. Nothing is by accident.

The four tribes as the heads of Israel are the representatives of four law-givers, in respect to civil law, and these four stand to represent the three forms of the church since the origin of the gospel church at the "breaking of the day," or at the rise of the United States, as the Israel of law. These law-givers are civil judges in Israel. They are the first, the seventh, the last, and the law-giver from "between the feet of Judah." The first as George Washington. or Joshua, was of Reuben, and stands to represent Ruth, or Elizabeth, or the daughter that followed the mother-in-law. The seventh was born in Levi or South Carolina, and is Andrew Jackson, who was the seventh judge in this Japhetic Israel. He was born of Levi, the tribe that gave the world a Moses, and his protest against the division of Israel is the protest of Moses, which will be removed after the demonstration is finished. If the judges of this Japhetic Israel be taken in their consecutive order, Andrew Jackson is the seventh; these will be, Washington, J. Adams, Jefferson, Madison, Monroe, J. Q. Adams, A. Jackson. It was at the seventh head of the Israel of Shem as judges, that God "solemnly protested" against any other king to Israel than his own written laws, as given by Levi, because Moses came of Levi. Andrew Jackson, the seventh in this land, protested against any other king than the written laws. The opposite judge, as the seventh, in the literal Israel to Andrew Jackson, in this land, was Abimilech.

The protest of God was against a forcible law, or king, as he stated what heavy burdens would be placed upon Israel by the departure from the written law. The protest of Andrew Jackson was to the same purport. That force that was represented by Abimilech, the seventh judge, has, at the close of the seven Northern judges, in this land, or at James Buchanan, come to the throne of Israel. Like the Abimilech of the Israel of Shem, he has done this by slaying seventy of his brethren, or excluding about that number from the seat of law, and like Abimilech, he has captured both Sarah, the law of gospel, which is the second time the law of gospel has been captured, and he has captured Rebecca the church of gospel. That he has done this ignorantly is all the truth, according to the types set in Abraham and Isaac, for this Abimilech did not know that these which he has captured were God's chosen, as the bride to the husband. This is God's method to show that he is the only king. While this seventh judge in this land, as Andrew Jackson, born of Levi, stands like Washington, the first born of Reuben, both to represent the civil law, neither have the bride to the husband. This Andrew Jackson takes the bride that Simeon, as Plymouth, the seventh son, held, standing for Congregational Orpah, or the scattered churches.

The bride is not with the diocesian Episcopal Ruth that holds to succession, as the mother-in-law, Naamah Nor is it with the scattered Orpah that holds to Presbyterian ordination. As John Wesley come from between these out of England as "the earth that helped the woman," so is the literal fact in the last and seventh civil head of this demonstrative Israel in the person of James Polk, who was born in Simeon, or North Carolina, between Reuben and Levi, and who was a Wesleyan Methodist. God's mean is between man's extremes. As in the settlement of this Japhetic Israel, the seventh or Puritan head of England, as Cromwell, settled the extreme North as Plymouth, and as the seventh head of Rome, as Napoleon Bonaparte, settled the extreme South, or Orleans territory, which two extremes stood to represent man in his double nature—the one as wholly a beast or literal being, and that he had no future existence, the other giving a spiritual application to every truth in God's book, and construing all things into the "Doing to others as ye would they should do to you," without the least regard to the civil arrangement of God's laws, so is the church of God between the two extremes of Ruth and Orpah. While there is no virtue in the imposition of the hands of the Bishop as Ruth would teach, yet it is not to be set aside as Orpah would teach. It is God's arrangement to give unity, vitality, and aggressive power to his church.

God used names, and tribes, and measures of times, and measures of numbers, and dates, and coincidents, in the Israel of Shem, to "seal the book," with its double laws for his double creature man. So in the Israel in the land of Japheth's enlargement over Shem, he uses the same things to "unseal the book." No man, nor all men, could ever have done it. Yet God, as an act of sovereignty, has been pleased to make "National Judah" worthy to "unloose the seals and open the book." No mortal, dead or living, is entitled to any credit for doing it. The ten kingdoms of West Rome are Ephraim in the land of Japheth. The United States stood for the two tribes, Benjamin and Judah. If Israel be transferred to this land, then the North is Ephriam, and the South is both Benjamin and Judah. The tribe of Judah in National Judah is Georgia. The law-giver from "between his feet" is Jefferson Davis, as the literal man to represent the head of civil law. His vice-head, as A. H. Stephens, is out of the tribe of Judah. Do these hold the same law that was first put up as a union of choice and as "States Rights?" Do these as heads of law hold the same law that ruled at the coming of the first son of Joseph or Manassah, or Kentucky, at which time Jerusalem began to be rebuilt? What says God's representative names? David as the civil law was the law of this restored Israel at its rise. This David came at the end of fourteen generations or heads of law, from Abraham, as gospel to David. This was the first anointing of David as the civil ruler. The great leaders to set up the law were Thomas Jefferson and Alexander Hambleton. The nation over which the law ruled made "Ham a servant of tribute." This law taught that the fugitive escaping from one tribe to another, should be rendered back. As this law returned to the South, it was to set the fourteen generations from David to the captivity, and also to annoint David the second time by National Judah. The heads of law at the end of "fourteen generations" are the same as at first, yet they are out of the tribe of Judah. These are Jefferson Davis and Alexander H. Stephens. This is done, not to change the husband or civil law, but in order to show who the bride to the husband is. While the heads of law to the civil stand for the seventh nation, each with seven heads, which is the sixth merged into the seventh, the church's head is also the seventh out of the tribe of Judah in National Judah.

The blessings of Jacob and Moses upon the tribe of Judah refer to him in both a national and a tribe sense, and as such he will be left till we consider all the tribes. The tribes are unity in the laws coming from Judah, as they are unity in the laws meeting in Joseph. Let us dispose of the other three heads as law-givers in Israel in the shortest way in connection with the prophecies of Jacob and Moses, in telling them for what they would stand in Israel. More ought in justice to be said of either one of these than shall be said of the three. Jacob said of Reuben, "thou art my first-born, my might and the beginning of my strength—the excellency of dignity and power Unstable as water, Reuben, thou shalt not excel, because thou wentest up to the thy father's bed, then defidest thou it: he went went up to my couch."

Reuben, the first-born, is the tribe chosen in this land to act that double part which the literal Israel of Shem acted in reference to the laws of God and the laws of nature. Reuben is the synopsis to Israel in this land. Reuben is Virginia—he has strength, might, power, dignity, yet he is wanting in stability. If Reuben taught "States Rights," he bound the nation to consolidation. If Reuben said "Freedom in religion," he had an established church. If Reuben was a slaveholder, he laid a prohibition upon his northwestern territory by the ordinance of 1787, that slavery should not go there, and he broke up the slave trade in 1808. If Reuben said, governments were by consent of the governed, he brought Zebulon, or Florida, without consulting the will of its inhabitants. If Reuben said all men were " Born free and equal," he did not act upon the declaration in holding Ham in bondage. Reuben is the only tribe in Israel that has been so unstable. Reuben is the tribe to act the double

THE MYSTERY FINISHED.

part on all questions concerning this Japhetic Israel. The other tribes are given to act out and show both the negative and positive parts in the double action of Reuben. This Reuben, though "unstable as water," is still "the excellency of power and dignity." He is also the strength of might. Suffice it to say, that the greatest statesmen in the nation, and the greatest jurists, and the greatest generals, came of Reuben.

Moses said "Let Reuben live and not die, and let not his men be few." Reuben is called "the Mother of States," and he has given more tone and standing to the nation than any other tribe, perhaps more than all the others combined. Of Reuben came Washington, "the Father of his Country." Of him came Jefferson, the second father, as the purchaser of the second half of the nation, and who is called the father of the doctrine of "States Rights," as the son of Reuben. Of Reuben came Madison, "the father of the Constitution." Of Reuben came Monroe, that brought the tribe of Zebulon. Of Reuben came Tyler, that brought Benjamin. Reuben cannot die while these names shall live. Reuben is "the excellency of dignity." He does not move with the haste of his more fiery brethren. If his son, as "States Rights," yet within the union, is imperilled by fiery and impetuous Levi of the South, it is the dignity of Reuben that restores the brother and calms the storm. If his son, as "Freedom in Religion," is imperiled by the storm that swept the North from side to side, in their resolves against the mother, Naamah, as Catholic Rome, again it was a son of Reuben that grappled with the storm and broke its force. When Israel had achieved the victory over her enemies and Deborah, the nurse of Rebecca, the gospel church sang of the victory, she said, "for the divisions of Reuben there were great searchings of heart," Israel's difficulties have been owing to the double dealing of Reuben. Let these suggested thoughts suffice for Reuben.

When Jacob came to bless Simeon and Levi, he united them. "Simeon and Levi are brethren." These have been brethren as church and State in Rome; they are again brethren in this land, as church and State united under Simeon, as the second son, or Plymouth colony, and Levi standing for all the scattered churches. In this land of Israel, in which the literal is given as the exponent of the sense, Simeon and Levi, as brethren, are simply Carolina. Jacob said of these brothers. "instruments of cruelty are in their habitation. O, my soul, come not thou into their secret; unto their assembly mine honor be not thou united! for in their anger they slew a man; in their self-will they digged down a wall." Cursed be their anger, for it was fierce, and their wrath, for it was cruel. I will divide them in Jacob, and scatter them in Israel."

As a piece of composition, this blessing is equal to any part of Job. It belongs to that class of writings found in nothing out of God's book. No conception of the human mind can add one word, nor can one be taken away. The cruelty of these brethren when united as church and State, their secret council, their want of honor, their fierce anger, their cruel wrath, and their digging down a wall that God had set up between them, is told in an unearthly strain in the fewest words by God's prophet. All the billingsgate of man cannot make one single addition to that that is here announced. The subject is exhausted. The long line of God's martyred witnesses rise up in review before the mind, reflecting upon the action of these brothers—the horrors of the inquisition, the tortured death by faggot and sword, the secret plotting on the night of the good Saint Bartholomew, the exhuming of the bones of God's martyred dead, and casting them upon the dung-hill, as unfit for the rights of sepulchre. How accurately all this was told by Jacob, thousands of years before it all came to pass. These brethren, in this land of Israel, are again united, and have been robbing and plundering the sacred mementoes to cover the dead. Their fierce anger and cruel wrath still attends them. "How long, O, Lord, wilt thou give the heritage of Jacob for a reproach?" "They shall be divided in Jacob and scattered in Israel." It is still a question of debate, whether Simeon, of the North, as Plymouth, or Simeon, of the South, as North Carolina, stood in the front to scatter Simeon, in the first work of this Japhetic Israel, to slay an "old man," as the "divine right of kings;" Levi, of the South, stands in the front to scatter both Simeon and Levi in the second work of this Israel to slay a "young man" as the divine right of numbers to rule without law. These tribes in this Israel stand in the front to oppose those laws of which they stood the types in Israel's past history. When Moses blesses the tribes he leaves out Simeon. As much is learned by the omission to do a thing as by the doing of it. That force for which Simeon stood, having been used to bring Israel to the law of Benjamin, there is no longer any use for Simeon. The Lord's Christ is Benjamin and Joseph; when these come, Simeon takes his departure. Joseph said, "Bring me Benjamin, and I will release Simeon."

Let us see what Moses said of Levi. His blessing upon Levi is in keeping with that of Jacob upon both Simeon and Levi. Moses said of Levi, which as a tribe, in this land, is

South Carolina, "Let thy Thummim and thy Urim be with thy holy one, whom thou didst prove at Massah, and with whom thou didst strive at the waters Meribah; who said unto his father and to his mother, I have not seen him; neither did he acknowledged his brethren, nor know his own children, for they have observed thy word and kept thy covenant. They shall teach Jacob thy judgments, and Israel thy law; they shall put incense before thee an whole burnt sacrifice upon thine altar. Bless, Lord, his substance and accept the work of his hands—smite through the the loins of them that rise against him, and of them that hate him, that they rise not again."

If that part remaining to be fulfilled concerning this tribe of Levi, shall be as accurately fulfilled as all the first part, then will the prophecy stand as one of the most exact and sublime ones in all God's book. If Levi gave the world a law-giver, in the person of Moses, in the Israel of Shem, it is the work of the Levi, in the land of Japheth, to bring the nation to the law thus given. Levi standing for the ceremonial law of the church, led Israel astray from the law of Moses, when in the person of Jeroboam, he appointed ignoble ones to the priesthood. Levi, as the church, united with Simeon in Rome, and in the persons of the Pope's, did the same thing. As Eve led Adam away from the law of God, so has it been with Levi. While Levi was separated from Simeon, in this land of Israel, both Simeon and Levi were "scattered" upon the doctrine of "States rights" and "freedom in religion." The wall that had been dug down by these brothers in Rome, was set up, and as the literal fact in this land is up with the symbolic, a dividing line was drawn between Simeon and Levi, as North and South Carolina. The action of Reuben, Simeon, Levi, Judah, and the whole nation, drove out this law that "scattered Simeon and Levi in the year 1821, by the Missouri Compromise line, and drove out the law of Moses for which the tribe of Benjamin stood, and drove out the tribe of Benjamin at the same time. As in the literal Israel, the absence of Moses forty days, was enough for Israel to depart from the teaching of Moses, and worship the golden calf of Aaron; so in the Japhetic Israel, the departure of the law of Moses for forty years made the whole nation to bow to the golden calf. As the literal Moses ground that calf to powder and sprinkled it upon the waters and told Israel to drink it," so the law of Moses in this land will grind that calf to powder, and the nation will drink it. Moses commanded the tribes to gird on their swords and go through Israel and smite all who had worshipped Aaron's calf. One tribe only followed the law of Moses, that tribe was Levi. The same truth applies to the tribe of Levi in this Japhetic Israel As in the Israel of Shem, this tribe drew the sword against brother and son, and all his kindred, and knew nothing but the law of God, so it is with him in this demonstrative Israel. Levi went into this fight upon his own hook; is Levi entitled to any credit for this? Not a word of it. It is God demonstrating to his creature man that his law is king.

This contest in Israel is required to show who is the bride among the seven churches to the law of Moses. As the literal Moses was gone forty years, and then returned with his literal wife, Zipporah, who was chosen from among the seven daughters of Reuel, so the law of Moses that left this land in 1821, and which is brought back by the tribe Levi, in 1861, is given to show not only what the husband is, but who is the bride to the husband. Leah was the bride with the civil law of England, as the husband at the coming of Levi. These are not God's husband and bride. At the birth of Levi, Leah said, "Now will my husband be joined to me." The law of Levi as the husband and the church law of Judah as the bride, are the laws of God, and both of these must come of Judah. These must be united upon the laws of God and not the laws of human kings. If the husband says, "Thou shalt not covet thy neighbors servant," the bride must say the same thing, "Servants be obedient to your masters."

The wife of Moses circumcised her son," or made him conform to the civil law of Moses, and threw it at the feet of Moses, saying, "Thou art to me a bloody husband." So the bride or church conforming to the law of Moses will find this law a bloody husband. The "Nahash," begotten by the disobedience of Adam and Eve, stands to oppose God and his laws. Through blood they are to triumph over this natural man. The bride of Moses was an Ethiopian woman; so the bride to the law of Moses must be a bride that recognizes the Ethiopian as a member of the church, and that hold him as "A servant of tribute." Aaron and Miriam may complain of this. It matters not. God is sovereign, and he will strike with leprosy all who oppose his action. God will choose his own queen. If it be little Esther, the hated Jewess, of whom no one thought, he has promised her the half of his kingdom—it is the soul half. The Ham-man, or natural man, may not like it. In order to prevent the union, this Ham-an may build his gallows very high. No; matter, the Mordicca at the gate will not bow to him. God has decreed his laws shall get upon the king's horse. Not only will Golioh be slain, but Uriah, the friend of David, and if the friend of David, the friend of God, must go in the front of the battle. Who is this Uriah? Episcopal Ruth and Congregational Orpha, are God's Uriah. Episcopal Washington and Presbyterian Jackson, who stands as their representatives in this contest, in which "Levi places whole burnt sacrifice upon the altar;" Bishop Leonidas Polk and Stonewall Jackson. Put Uriah in the front of the battle. The bride to the law of Moses must come of the tribe of Judah. The bride will bear the name of both the first judge of the seventh head of law, and the first apostle of the seventh head of gospel. Who are these? Joshua and Andrew. These are Joshua Saul, and James Andrew. Are these out of the right tribes to build the Tabernacle? We shall see before we are done.

It is the tribe of Levi that holds the "Urim and Thummim" that reflects the divine will. These are light and perfection. The Thummim and Urim worn by the priests was intended to reflect the divine will. The will of God was reflected upon it in all questions of the literal Israel, until God raised up prophets to take the place of the Thurmim and Urim. The tribe of Levi in this land who has an inheritance, because Joseph becomes his substitute, is the tribe chosen to reflect the divine will. This tribe in Israel took more pains to have Ham orally taught and instructed in the law of gospel, than any other tribe in Israel. It was his own William Capers that provided the catachism for Ham's benefit. This tribe has never been willing, like the other tribes, to yield the greater to the less. If the law of Moses for the government of man collided with the law of union, when the one or the others had to yield, he always followed Moses rather than the law of man. In this respect he holds the Thurmim and Urim. The two tribes of Levi and Judah, are the only two of the first settlement of this Japhetic Israel, that were among the first seven that put up the Southern Confederacy. These two stand for Moses and Christ, and are the two wings with which the cheribim covered his face. "With twain he covered his face, with twain he covered his feet, and with twain he did fly." Let these thoughts suffice for Levi. Judah is the tribe with which Leah was going to "praise the Lord," and as he gives the national name, as to him all the tribes are to "bow down," we will leave Judah and pass to the consideration of the two servant maid's four children.

The two of Rachel are Dan and Naphtali. The first born is Dan, and is Tennessee. God's laws are doubled according to the double prophecy of Noah, or the double covenants set in Abraham. The Israel of law, and the Israel of both law and gospel, have respect to the double nature of man. There are agreeing correspondents in Israel and direct opposites. Cain and Seth are agreeing correspondents, while the "Nahash," begotten of Adam and Eve, are the direct opposite; Shem and Japheth are agreeing correspondents, while Ham is the direct opposite; Isaac and Ishmael are agreeing correspondents, while Babylon and Egypt are the opposite; Esau and Jacob are both agreeing and opposing correspondents; Joseph and Benjamin are agreeing correspondents, while the ten brethren of Joseph are his opposites; Rachel finds an agreeing correspondent in Leah, while in Jezebel she finds a "woman that rides a scarlet colored beast." The double types of the Israel from Shem, as twelve patriarchs and twelve apostles, will find a double settlement in the Israel of Japheth before Israel will find both his agreeing and opposing correspondents. The laws are only perfect when without the failure of a "jot or tittle" they come to Moses for the body and Christ for the soul or church.

The whole lot of children that make the settlement of the Israel of law, in this land of Japheth's enlargement, were Leah's, as Reuben and Judah, or the first, and the last were Leah's. If all the tribes and all the churches be Leah's, how can any part be Rachel's? That latitude which Leah has claimed in those extremes which she has used, as expressed by her son Reuben, such as "governments are by consent and religion is free," has included all manner of governments and religion, and in doing this has also included those laws for which Rachel, as the word of God, stands. A second settlement was necessary to show what things of the first were Rachel's and what Leah's. The joint holding of the husband after the seven years of war, or the seven years of service, for both Rachel and Leah is intended to show at which tribes the law is approved, and at which it is not approved because it is Leah's. The two of Rachel that were set up at Philadelphia as summaries of laws to all the rest, were all that she claimed in the first settlement of Israel. These were by that act designated as the heads to be followed in finding the laws of Rachel as husband and bride.

The first born of the four that were territories, settled by the other tribes in the second settlement of this demonstrative Israel was Tennessee, and is in agreement with the first born of Rachel's maid servant. Rachel said at the birth of this child to Jacob, "Give me children or I die." Jacob replied, "Am I in the stead of God that I can give you children?" Rachel, standing for the laws of God, had not had one single tribe among the whole twelve at first born, and as such, the laws of God, for which she stood, would die in this land if thus it should continue. The reply of Jacob shows the nature of the prophecy. It is about this in substance: Rachel, I move as "God the Holy Ghost" will move in Israel, and you move as the laws of God, and you cannot have children until the time comes for us to set the types of Israel's history. Rachel's maid servant pressed hard upon her knees and brought forth a son. At his birth, Rachel said, "The Lord hath judged me," and she called his name Dan. Jacob said of Dan, "Dan shall judge his people as a tribe in Israel." This judging of his people by the tribe of Dan, could not refer to the first Israel in this land, because Dan was then a part of this Simeon which belonged to the tribes of whom Judah was the last. This prophecy of Jacob must then refer to the second settlement of Israel.

Rachel said, "The Lord hath judged me." Jacob said Dan should judge for himself. How did Dan judge in this matter? Dan submitted to the voice of the people about whether he would come with Israel, or go to the "virgin daughter of Babylon." The Lord's judging and Dan's judgment are used as synonymous terms between Rachel and Jacob. Dan is (perhaps) the only tribe in Israel that submitted his case to the voice of the whole people. What then, as a principle of law to govern Israel, is learned from the action of the tribe of Dan? The voice of the people in their tribe capacity, when, according to the law of Moses, is the voice of God. This was the principle of law that ruled in Israel, before Israel departed from it by following the law of nature. When David, as the civil law, was annointed king in Israel, it was upon the doctrine of "local charters," "States rights." Sarah, the law of gospel, was restored by Egypt to Abra-Ham with all that Abraham had. This was at the rise of the United States. All the tribes held Ham to be a servant in the stead of Canaan, the son to literal Israel, according to the second covenant made in Abra-Ham. In violation of this law of God and Moses, Reuben said, "Governments are by the consent of the governed," and "All men are born free and equal." It is to no use for Reuben to say there was a spirit to the law not expressed in the declaration. God will be honored not only in the spirit of the law, but in the letter of its reading. Had Reuben said, "Governments are by consent of the sons of Japheth, when taken in their tribe capacity, provided they are in agreement with the law of Moses, it would have been the truth. Man can no more violate the political or soul laws of God and go unpunished, than he can violate the laws of gravitation. In this respect the iniquities of the fathers will be visited upon the children, in this present state of man, to the third and fourth generation." God moves with a trinity in all things. At the "breaking of the day," or reformation, the three names of Luther, Zuingle, Calvin, are a trinity. The same is true in reference to John Wesley, Charles Wesley, and Whitfield, at the "cleansing of the sanctuary." These are as executive, legislative and judicial. These are a trinity, because of the opinions they hold or represent. The same is true in reference to the three men as Lincoln, Douglas, Breckinridge, which were the candidates for judge in this land at the division of Israel. Let us glance at the application of the laws which these represent to the characters for which they stand. Luther follows the letter of the reading of the law, "This is my body. Zuingle gives the spirit to the letter, and says it is to be received as any other symbol, such as, "I am the door," "I am the vine," &c. Calvin stands to this spirit and letter as the elect holding the laws as the elect for the government of men, in this life, while the elect of the future life are those who themselves choose to elect. Turning to the civil representatives of this land—Lincoln holds the letter of the reading, all men are born equal; Douglas holds the spirit to the letter, and urges that the author of the declaration, in the declaration prefers a charge against the mother country, for producing "domestic insurrections," which shows a spirit to the letter not contained in the letter. This antagonism between letter and spirit drives Breckinridge to set up the elect that is to combine both spirit and letter to make them harmonize the one with the other. A simple glance at these great truths is all that can be indulged in.

The tribe of Dan, the son of Rachel, is given to show that the voice of the people, is the voice of God in their tribe capacity, when according to the fundamental law to govern Israel. This fundamental law acknowledges Ham as a servant throughout the whole boundary of Israel. This law does not force him as a servant where his labor is of no use, yet should he escape to such place or tribe, that tribe cannot violate the law of Moses in not recognizing him in his true relation as a "servant of tribute," and in rendering him back to the one whose "money he is by the law of God."

Jacob said, "Dan shall be a serpent by the way, an adder in the path, that biteth the horse heels so that the rider shall fall backwards." The geographical position of the tribes will, in every instance, be found in agreement with the prophecy. Dan is the only tribe in Israel that is geographically like an adder, long and narrow, stretching a

great ways across the whole of Israel. While this is a literal truth, that principle of law, which makes him an adder, is the principle that he shall judge his people for himself.
The one man power, as kings, would deprive Dan of this right. The same truth, as the divine right of numbers, exercised by the other tribes, would deprive him of the same right. In the first case, Saul would claim that he was the "Lord's annointed" and had the right to rule. In the second case, the virgin daughter of Babylon would claim that God had given her the power to rule Dan, and that as such she was "the Lord's annointed," to rule Dan upon her own interpretation of the law of God. These will each rule according to the times appointed. God says Dan shall judge for himself, and that those who say otherwise "Shall fall backwards." Jacob uses a parenthesis in blessing Dan, "I have waited for thy salvation, O, Lord!" This would indicate that powerful efforts would be made to seduce Dan to revoke his judgment that determined him upon the side of Israel, but these efforts would not succeed. God would keep him until he would save him. Moses said of Dan, "He shall leap from Bashan." Dan is the only tribe in Israel that gave an overwhelming majority to hold on to Bashan, or Asdod, and then suddenly gave a larger vote to come to Israel—he come with a leap. When Deborah sings of the victory of Israel, she asks, "why dwelt Dan in ships?" Dan's governor has taken ship and left. If, out of Reuben, the first son of Leah came, five of the seven judges of this wing of Israel, out of Dan, the first son of Rachel, came the other two. Out of the tribe of Dan, in literal Israel, came the last regular Judge of Israel—his name was Samson; the Philistines led him about for a while, but his strength returned again. This Samson, in this Israel, is out of Dan, and while he is "that great prince that standeth up for Israel," he is " the eighth-seventh revived head of Israel was Andrew Jackson, the seventh; Andrew Johnson, is the seventh revived head; he is the revived head of unity in Israel, but not of the laws of unity. Let this suffice for Dan, as we need not speculate.

The three territories of Mississippi, Alabama and Arkansas were contemporary as territories in this Israel. It is left to the literal facts in connection with the prophecies to settle the claims of these as to which of the two mothers, as Rachel and Leah, they belong. It will be seen that these are made so plain there can be no difficulty in determining. The tribe of Naphtali, standing for the second son of Rachel's maid, is Alabama. At the birth of this tribe, Rachel said, " With great wrestling have I wrestled with my sister, and I have prevailed." It was in this tribe, for the first time since the world began, that God's form of civil law for the body, and church law for the soul, ever met in a national sense. These laws met as civil and ceremonial in Moses, and in the nation of Moses; they met symbolically on David, they met in truth on "the Christ;" they met in a civil government and in a collective church in Naphtali, in the year 1861, as a place and a character. Rachel as the word or laws of God "prevailed." The laws which met symbolically on Moses, the sixth head of law, or on Christ, the sixth head of gospel, met in Naphtali, as the sixth tribe in this Japhetic Israel. These met by a union of the seventh head as judges, and the seventh as the apostles with the heads of both out of Judah, as the law-giver in this Japhetic Israel. These were the seventh nation, each with seven heads, and the seventh church, and they are David the seventh son, and Bathsheba the seventh daughter; the head of the civil was Jefferson Davis, and the head of the church was Bishop James Andrew, the same apostle, first chosen at the seventh head as "the apostles." The civil law-giver was from between the literal feet of the literal Judah, while the "Shiloh," the head of the church, was out of the tribe of Judah. Nobody is to be praised or blamed. It is not you but the God that made the world, trying to "save life, and not to destroy." This union could never have been formed so long as the husband and the bride were antagonistic to each other. The laws of God, as written in his word, and which are Rachel, had to become " the head stone of the corner," and not the "Nahash," with Cain and Seth, or Ham, with Shem and Japheth. If Moses said Canaan should serve Japheth, Paul affirmed it, and for the bride to teach "slavery is a great evil," and to inquire "what shall be done for the exterpation of slavery," was the bride taking council of the "Nahash," and not of the laws of God. When the bride published her laws to the world, in conformity to Moses, and the husband also conformed, " Rachel prevailed." This was done by both parties in the year 1861.

The civil government put up at Montgomery, Ala., by the seven tribes, that move with the seven heads of Israel, and which stands as "the seven eyes of God," and the church cleansed at the end of 2400 years, by the coming of Andrew out of the tribe of Judah, are in substance the same as the two sons of Rachel, "Benjamin and Joseph." These are the children over which "Rachel weeps," and will not be comforted because " they are not." The times for these to suffer "reproach " are not yet numbered; the measures are not yet full for these to prophecy in sackcloth and ashes; as in the dividing sisters, Mary and Elizabeth, Naomi and Ruth, Catholic Mary and Protestant Elizabeth, God made Elizabeth a negro trader; so in the division of the gospel church in this land which takes its date from Judah, God made Bishop James Andrew, who was the only Bishop in the Southern wing of the church, a slave holder. Esdras asked the Almighty why he went into the field, to change the temple or house to a woman? The reply was, "I go where no man's building is," that is, "I do it myself; I will build it in my own way, and by my own laws; the rejected stone shall become the head stone of the corner." If God says, "Ham the father of Canaan, the son, shall serve Japheth," men need not soften the word slavery down by "domestic institutions." It is against the laws of nature that God and his laws are at war. The light of nature is his exponent. Ham is a beast in all lands without Shem or Japheth to help him rise above the beast. God says he is not a beast, but was made in his image; that image is so marred that, of himself, he can never rise above the beast, nor can he ever rise by understanding a complex law, when God has demonstrated it; yet Abra-Ham must heir the world; this he cannot do while Ham is a beast; this he could never do if Ham is left to himself, hence he must be made a " servant of servants," This appears as the means of Heaven's ordaining to bring Ham to the covenants set in Abraham as law and gospel. Jacob said of Naphtali, "Naphtali is a hind let loose, he giveth goodly words." The hind is the symbol of a traveling, moving clergy. As the hind scales hights, and leaps vales, so with the clergy heading the gospel church. This hind could never be "let loose" and give "goodly words" so long as his church law contradicted Moses. When he ordered it all blotted out in the year 1858, and when it was done, in truth, by the year 1861, all of which times (as will be seen) are measured, then Naphtali "gave goodly words." Moses said of Naphtali, " O, Naphtali, satisfied with favor, and full with the blessing of the Lord, possess thou the South and the West." It is enough. Rachel prevails, and Moses says, "full with the blessing of the Lord." Rachel's servant ought to be satisfied with this. The " Book of God," in its two departments, as civil and soul laws, has come together. These have met in a South land. The same place in which Jacob found his " father's house." That compromise line which was required to bring the laws together, will not now be needed for the West. The demonstrated laws of God will become their substitute when the " scales falls from the eyes of Saul or Benjamin, of Tarsus" by the shining of a great light. This Saul will see that it was an act of sovereignty alone with God to transfer the government from Saul to David, or from Benjamin to Judah or Joseph; this Joseph may go in prison, and they may "put his feet in fetters." The literal Joseph was two years in prison; these as types will find their anti-type. Men have no idea of letting this "dreamer," as the laws of God, rule them. No matter—it will go just as God has marked it out; there will not be one mistake or one accident. God told Moses how it would all go and how it would stand in "the last days." There has not been one mistake for four thousand years, and it will keep moving that same way. This world belongs to the son of God, and neither the "Nahash" of Adam, nor the Ham of Noah shall hold it; it is God's decree; the sword must reign till all things are given to the rightful owner. The tribe of Naphtali is the only tribe in this Israel that was admitted into this second settlement of Israel without one word of dispute about Ham. Rachel "prevailed." We must pass over the reasons for this. The two children of Leah's maid servant are Gad and Asher; Gad is Arkansas, and Asher is Mississippi.

At the birth of Gad, Leah said a "troop cometh." The tribe of Gad was the dividing tribe in Israel. The half way was between Naphtali, as the sixth, and Gad, as the seventh. This division made the balance in the literal Israel an equal one, as six upon one side, and six upon the other. The tribe of Gad, in this respect, stands as the "doubting Thomas" among the apostles. As the second Southern judge in this land bought the second half of Israel, as the doubting Thomas Jefferson, and stands to represent the second half of Israel, so it is with the tribe of Gad; Gad is the first tribe in Israel to represent the second half of Israel. The tribe of Ephraim as Missouri, is only a half tribe; the tribe of Benjamin, or Texas, is after that of Gad; as the tribe of Gad is the tribe of equilibrium in Israel, so was he admitted into the union upon the doctrine of "equilibrium" in government. This, as a principle of human government, is the doctrine of Leah, and not that of Rachel. The sword must forever remain the arbiter in the world, if it is to be governed by the changing laws of equilibrium. Human opinions will jostle that equilibrium, and the sword will be drawn to adjust the balance. Rachel, standing for God's written laws, knows nothing of equilibrium, or balance in power. The tribe of Gad likewise stands to represent the second half of Israel—the troop made up of the one half because the balance is lost comes against the other half.

Jacob said of Gad, "A troop would overcome him, but

he would overcome at the last." This is only a different form of presenting the "two witnesses that were to be killed," and yet they were to stand upon their feet again. The same fact is presented in the gallows Haman built for Mordicai, and upon which he gets himself.

Moses said of Gad, "Blessed be he that enlargeth Gad." The tribe of Gad, like that of Ephraim, set the western boundary of Israel. The Missouri Compromise not only divided Israel North and South, but set the western boundary of Israel, (Thomas H. Benton,) as this compromise was required for a special work to cut off the demonstrative Israel; after it is done, Gad will be "enlarged." Moses said of Gad: that he was seated in a portion of the law-giver, and he provided the first part for himself. There are two law-givers to Israel, these are Ephraim and Judah. Judah is Georgia, Ephraim is Missouri. This prophecy is doubly true in reference to these law-givers. If it was forty years from Judah to Philadelphia; so it is forty years from Ephraim in 1821, to Naphtali, the place of Rachel triumph. If Judah gives the national name to Israel, the tribe of Gad was first seated in that part of Israel that first crossed the Jordan. If Ephraim be the law-giver, he was a part of the territory of Ephraim. Gad is the only tribe in which the prophecy is doubly fulfilled. Moses said of Gad, he "dwelleth as a lion and teareth the arm with the crown of the head." Gad, the servant of Leah, holds to her the relation that Dan does to Rachel. It was said of Dan, "He is a lion's whelp." It is said of Gad, "He dwelleth as a lion." If the principle of Dan which says, "Dan shall judge his people as a tribe," is God's lion to rule the world; so Gad, standing to represent the second half of Israel, is the half to represent that wing of Israel in which the principle is contended for, in contrast with the other half that claims to rule by the force of numbers. Out of the half represented by Gad shall come the judge that holdeth the crown to tear the arm of power wielded by the opposing half.

We pass to learn what is taught by the second son of Leah's maid servant. This son is Asher and stands for Mississippi. At the birth of Asher, Leah said, "Happy am I, for the daughters will call me blessed." That which had been as the husband with Leah in the first settlement of Israel is at the birth of Asher changed to the "daughters." These daughters were going to organize another husband with its head out of Asher, and hence "the daughters will call me blessed. Jacob said in blessing Asher, "out of Asher," that head which the daughters were going to praise Leah for, and which was to come from "between the feet of

Judah," was to come out of the tribe of Asher, and the government over which he was to rule was to set up in Naphtali, as the other foot of Judah. Jacob said, "His bread shall be fat, and he shall yield royal dainties." He is the man chosen to represent God's form of civil law, as the husband to the bride, and when this fact is established the good that will come to the world will be "royal dainties." Moses said, "Let Asher be blessed with children, let him be acceptable to his brethren, and let him dip his foot in oil." "Thy shoes shall be iron and brass, and as thy day is, so shall thy strength be."

How far individual men in this Israel will be used for the laws they are given to represent, cannot be known till it is finished. As in typical Israel, many persons were used before the ideas for which they stand are perfected, so in this Japhetic Israel it may require many different persons to perfect the ideas for which they stand. The union of God's laws that meet in Naphtali, the civil head of which comes from the tribe of Asher, are as "iron and brass." These are more unchangeable than the laws of the "Medes and Persians." They are God's legs of iron to break up all human laws, and as they will cover the world, "Asher will be blessed with children."

Why is the tribe of Asher Leah's and not Rachel's? This tribe represents a division in Israel, whereas Rachel has no division. While the man of Asher holds the civil law of Israel, he does not represent the law of the soul. Ruth is the servant of Leah and not that of Rachel; Ruth is the church of England, Rachel is John Wesley, and then James Andrew, out of Judah. Will this head out of Asher save Israel? As the Earth at first was divided between Jokton and Eber, so is this land of Israel divided between Eber and Asher. God's prophet says, "Asher shall not save us." Balaam, the prophet of the natural man, who had his eyes open, says of Asher and of Eber, "Ships from the coast of Chittim shall afflict Asher and carry him away captive. These shall in like manner carry Eber away, and he shall perish forever." This is in keeping with "the troop that was to overcome Gad, yet in the end he was to overcome." It is like to the rider of Dan that was to fall backwards; it is the same with Levi, "Strike through the loins of them that rise up against him, that they rise not again." It is remarkable that in the last contest of the laws of God with the laws of man, that the Israel chosen to represent the laws should have to go over the whole history of Israel.

Let these thoughts suffice for the four sons of the maid servants to Rachel and Leah. If Leah divides Israel with her son Asher, Rachel scatters Israel with her son Dan; if Leah teaches the doctrine of equilibrium in government with her son, Gad, Rachel shows the union of the laws of God with her son, Naphtali; Dan and Naphtali are to Rachel as Benjamin and Joseph; Asher and Gad are to Leah as Reuben and Simeon.

We come now to consider the two tribes of Leah, given to show who is a servant of tribute according to the divine law, and who is not. These are Issachar and Zebulon, or Louisiana and Florida. Louisiana is the tribe Issachar, and is the first tribe begotten with a bargain and sale between Rachel and Leah. In order to show the nature of this transaction, it is stated that Reuben, the son of Leah, went out into the fields in the days of wheat harvest and found mandrakes, which mandrakes Rachel requested Leah to give her, saying, " Give me your son's mandrakes." Leah told Rachel, "Thou hast taken my husband, and would you now take my son's mandrakes." Rachel said, " Give me your son's mandrakes, and he shall be with thee to-night." Leah went out in the field that evening to meet Jacob, and told him he must be with her to-night, and the child begotten by this transaction, Leah called Issachar, saying, "The Lord hath given me my hire." When Jacob come to bless this tribe he said, "Issachar is a strong ass, couching down between two burdens, he saw that rest was good, and the land that it was pleasant, and he bowed his shoulder to bear and became a servant to tribute."

This is the only time, among all the tribes born of Leah, that she ever had Jacob as " God the Holy Ghost," for a husband. At the birth of the tribe of Judah, she was going to " praise the Lord." This action, in literal fact, has precedence over either of the children belonging to the maid servants, except the tribe of Dan, according to the manner in which Jacob blesses them, yet they have been considered according to the order of the birth of each, and not according to the order of the blessing. This tribe stands for the Louisiana purchase, in this Israel, and in using a literal land to represent human actions, characters and principles of government, the child begotten is Ham the servant of tribute; he is that child begotten in the Japhetic Israel that changed Abram as law with the first covenant in Judah with Canaan, the son of Ham, to Abra-Ham, the father of Canaan. In the Israel of Shem, he was subjugated and made a servant of tribute. In the Israel of Japheth he was to be begotten by a bargain and sale, according to the literal prophetic act of Leah and Rachel. This is in agreement with the teaching of Isaaih. Speaking of the restored

Japhetic Israel, he uses the following language: (We give the substance,) "Strong men, the merchandise of Ethiopia, and the Sabeans, men of statue; they shall come over to thee, in chains shall they come, and they shall fall down before thee, saying God is with thee, and they shall be thine, and there is no other God but the God of thee, who thus decrees."

Reuben, laid a tax upon the wheat fields and the tobacco fields that he might gather tythes for his mother, Leah, in days when he had an established religion. As Rachel intended to change this method of gathering tythes according to the teachings of the New Testament, "Let each one give," she asked Leah, the established church, to "give" her these tythes. It is evident from what Leah then said, that Rachel had the husband or civil government that scattered Levi. This announcement is made at the Louisiana purchase in 1803-4. It is also evident that the African Slave Trade was then carried on while Rachel had the husband. Reuben had attempted to break it up since he defiled himself by the ordinance 1787. Simeon, as God's agent, stood to oppose him. Leah got possession of the husband by the year 1808. This was right, as by that time enough of Ham had been brought over for a demonstrative purpose. A double action was to be had; this had respect to Ham as a servant of tribute, and also to the method of collecting tythes by the church. The whole action is prophetic.

Leah met Jacob coming in the field. If Isaac met Rebecca coming in the field, it was the prophetic sign that the gospel church would date its rise with preaching in the field. "I go where no man's building is." If "Red Esau" was a man of the field, he was a roving hunter. If Sarah and Rebecca were both "fair women," it is because they stand for gospel given to the fair or Japhetic race. If in the case of Issachar, the servant, Leah, met Jacob coming in the field, it is the prophetic sign that the place for the character begotten was the field for labor as the "servant of tribute," that is, he is not a mechanic, he is not a merchant, but he is merchandise; he is not a professor, he is not a lawmaker. It was in the evening Leah met Jacob, to show he worked all the day. Leah said, "the Lord hath give me my hire." Jacob tells what that hire is. Issachar saw that the land was pleasant. This servant finds no pleasant land in all the world only as the servant of tribute to Shem and Japheth. This is his history, affirmed by the light of nature as God's exponent of his truth. Why does he find no pleasant land? His love of rest is too great. It is a question not easily determined whether it is more difficult to get Shem and Japheth to refrain from labor on the seventh day than it is to get Ham to labor six days in the seven. If God intends to be the master of the one party by the sword and by his demonstrated truth to their understanding, he forces it upon them to master the other, so as to bring the whole to one single law. Abraham, the representative of the laws of God, must take the world, " possessor of heaven and earth."

Let us now look at this question in the light in which God presents them to the understanding of men in his own explanation of his own truth.

The trinity of " Father, Son and Holy Ghost " is as the trinity of law, gospel and the union of the two. These are represented by Abraham, Isaac, and a union of the two in Jacob. The substitutes of these in a literal or political sense are Shem, Ham and Japheth. Isaac, the second person, stands as the " Son." As the Son, he is the " Eli-as " the God servant, to save. Ham, the second person, is the Isaac-er This is his name, and it is Isaac-er. This Isaac-er is " the ass," as the opposite of the Eli-as. This ass is the servant of tribute. If the Eli-as couches between two burdens, they are beneath the two laws of God to save the world as civil and soul laws, or body and soul. If the Isaac-er, as a strong ass, " couches between two burdens," they are God's two curses : " cursed is the ground, and cursed is Canaan, or Ham, or Isaac-er—a servant of servants shall he be to his brethren."

As the literal in this land is up with the symbolic, that literal tribe, as Louisiana, for which he stands, is divided into two parts by the Mississippi river, to represent the double curse or the two burdens. This is the only tribe thus divided.

This important question does not stop here. The learning one symbolic truth opens the way to another, and it is by finding out these symbols that the book of God can be made as readable as any other book. " Issachar is an ass," and this ass is a " servant of tribute," in contrast with the servant to atone, or save, or enlighten. This ass " bowed his shoulder to bear, and became a servant of tribute." The Christ, upon whom the laws of God met, rode into Jerusalem upon an " ass, the foal of an ass." The nation of the Christ in the land of Japheth's enlargement over Shem sets up the laws for which Jerusalem stood as Benjamin and Judah, by riding " the ass, the servant of tribute." Saul, the first king of the literal Israel by the will of man, following the Nahash and not the law of God, was made king while in pursuit of his father's asses. Saul was made king in this land while in pursuit of his father's asses or servants.

Abra-ham is law, and was law in this land when all the tribes held the ass as a servant of tribute. This law for which Abraham stood was at the end of the seventh head as judges from either wing of this Israel, whether as James Polk or James Buchanan, changed into a law of force, and it became Saul, and this was done while Saul was in search of his father's asses. This Saul came out of the tribe of Benjamin in the Israel of Shem. He came out of National Benjamin in this Japhetic Israel, though with the tribe of Benjamin in National Judah. The seventh head as Jas. Polk closed law with National Judah. Law with him, like the literal Abraham, went through the land and landed at the Pacific Ocean. Then it was Saul came in the shape of the "Wilmot Proviso," which said to Judah, you shall have no more territory for your asses to work. At the end of the seventh head, from national Benjamin, as James Buchanan, this Saul came from national Benjamin, and not only from national Benjamin, but from between the tribes with which Reuben defiled himself by the ordinance of 1787. The Israel from Shem still claimed Abraham for their father, notwithstanding every departure made from the law for which Abraham stood, so with the Israel of Japheth, they still claim to be seed of Abraham, without respect to the law for which Abraham stood. The literal Saul left the word of God, and went to the "witch of Endor," to learn the divine will. The witch of Endor is the symbol of the "spirit rappers" in this Israel. The end of Saul was tragical, he was killed by his armor-bearer, and fell upon his own sword. It was an act of sovereignty to transfer the kingdom from Saul to David, or from Benjamin to Judah. By force Saul said it should not be done. That force for which he contended was his armor-bearer, and according as man sows, so he shall reap is the law of God. Facts stand like mountains in the way, but as nobody is to blame, only that God chooses thus to prove to his poor creature man, his right to rule him, we will touch lightly. When all are guilty, none have the right to throw stones. It was said to Saul, "Your father's asses are found, but come thou and rule over us." The Missouri Compromise line in this Israel found the father's asses in national Judah and without Simeon or Saul, to drive Israel as God's whip, the truth that God set out to demonstrate, would never have been learned. When Abraham went to offer Isaac, that is, when law went to offer both law and gospel, he rode an ass. When the nation of law in this land offers the nation of both law and gospel, like Abraham it rides "the ass." The daughter of Caleb, representing Judah, lit off of her ass, saying, " Father thou hast given me a South land, give me springs of water." Caleb told her she should have "both the upper and the nether spring." This ass off of which this daughter has lit in this land is "the servant of tribute.

Samson, the last judge in Israel, and which stood as the summary of all the judges, the same as Joshua was the synopsis, said, "Heaps upon heaps have I slain with the jaw bone of an ass." Heaps upon heaps has this Samson slain in this Israel with jawing over the ass. When Samson became weary and was very thirsty, there came up a spring in the jawbone, with the water of which he slaked his thirst; Samson's riddle solves itself in this land. Out of this bitter there will come a sweetness, and out of this weakness there will come strength, and out of this thirst or desert, springs of water will break out. The light is shining, though the darkness does not yet comprehend it. " That determined on must be accomplished."

This servant of tribute whom Jacob said was an ass is a man, and he speaks with the voice of a man. When Balaam went the second time to curse Israel, he rode an ass. Baal is the God of the natural man, and he is the law of nature or the Nahash. Balak is the king of the natural man, and Balaam is his prophet, he prophesies according to the laws of nature; the prophets of God prophecy according to the laws of God. Balaam says, "All men are equal." God's laws and God's prophets say they are not. Balaam will be forced to the truth before he is done according to the pattern set him in his arch-type. When Balaam was sent the second time to curse Israel or the second nationality of Israel, he rode an ass. As he was riding along, the ass saw an angel in the path and refused to go, whereupon Balaam smote the ass three times. The ass remonstrated against Balaam, and said to him, "Have I not been thine ass upon which thou hast ridden, and when have I disobeyed you, and now these three times has thou smitten me?" The ass of Balaam ran him up to where two ways met and mashed his foot against the wall. The ass is the talking servant; this servant says to Balaam, "Have I not been thy servant to labor for you? Have I not contributed to your wealth and to the building of your great cities, and have kept nothing but the land upon which I labor for your benefit? When you wanted promotion to honor, you have ridden me. When we wanted representation in the national law, you smote us and gave us only three-fifths. When we wanted territory to work, you denied it, and said we should have no more. Now you have given us our freedom, and have thus taken us from our normal position in which we had a master to care for us. These three times has thou smitten us. If we are left in this relation we will become exterminated. In doing this you have overthrown one law of Israel as 'States rights,' 'local charters,' and have made it all consolidation. Between these you will find the two cannot be made to agree upon your notions, and you will get your foot mashed."

There is no need to enlarge the subject in this particular. The second covenant, which God set with Abraham, was in view of his offering Isaac upon the altar. Isaac is to Abraham as soul to body. If the question be considered in its theological aspect, every living man is required to offer his Isaac upon the altar. He must take his natural law or natural religion, and bring it to the law of God. This law teaches "Ye must be born again." In this offering he is not to confer with flesh and blood, but he must do as did Abraham, in offering Isaac. If man waits till he understands the philosophy of how his supernatural part can be born again, he will never offer his Isaac upon the altar; like Abraham, he must do it because God says so. It may seem to be the death of him to do it, but by faith it must be done. Instead of its proving the death of his Isaac, it will only be the death of the ram caught by two horns, as the laws of the natural man, or Nahash that is in every man. It is the placing of the Ham that is in him upon the altar.

This is an individual matter, and is the theological part of the question. With the work of the sons of Aaron, we pretend not to meddle, yet one remark in this connection may be required. As faith is the principle of justification in placing Isaac upon the altar, unless it be kept as an active principle, Isaac ceases to be offered. If ceremonies become the substitute, it is Hager and her son usurping the place of Sarah and her son, and it is declared Hager and her son shall not be heir with the son of Sarah. We only follow God's symbols, and pretend not to dictate to those whom God calls to teach his truth.

As the history of the individual man is the history of Israel in his political and soul relations, the political nation for which Abraham stands is called upon to offer Isaac upon the altar. This Isaac is the laws of the nation which met on "the Christ," the Isaac of God. As the laws cannot exist without a subject for their action, there must be component bodies in which they do exist. That the laws may exist, as in "mystical Babylon," when the woman was hid in the convent of Rome, is true. They existed only as a hidden light, without any organized bodies for the laws' action. A nation taking the kingdom is a nation of component parts, organized upon the principles of laws that constitute the kingdom. That nation is the Isaac among the nations, and also the Isaac of Abra-ham. If the laws that make the kingdom teach in both departments that the literal Ham is a "servant of tribute" in offering the laws that make Isaac, it follows that Ham must also be offered with the laws. The service which the laws demand from Ham must cease while Isaac is upon the altar. The symbolic action demands the offering. When the ram is caught by two horns and becomes the substitute for the laws of God that met in Isaac, the laws of the natural for both civil and church will give place to the laws of God for which Isaac or Abra-ham stands. Will this restore Ham to his true relations as a servant of tribute? So the types affirm, "It will bring the laws out of Babylon the same as the two tribes of the literal Israel came from Babylon, or the same as the Book of God for which the two tribes stood, came out of "mystical Babylon." In the first case, the two tribes, Benjamin and Judah, standing for law and gospel, brought the men and maid servants with them out of the literal Babylon. In coming from the "mystical Babylon," when Sarah the law of gospel was restored to Abraham with all that Abraham had, at the rise of the Israel of law as twelve tribes given to Japheth, or in the United States, not only was the book of two laws restored as the two tribes were restored, but Ham, as a servant of tribute, was also restored. Macauly says: "Moral causes noiselessly effaced the distinction of master and slave in England." If he had said, the confessional of the "man of sin standing in the temple of God, and making out as if he were God," by following the laws of nature, and not the laws of God, effaced the distinction of master and slave, he would probably have come nearer the truth. Every effort that God puts forth to bring Israel to his laws, shows the normal place of Ham to be that of a servant of tribute. The movements of the literal Abraham are the movements of "God the Father." Abraham is the greatest slaveholder, perhaps, that the Bible has in it. He is God's type of his own laws, once as Abram, and once as Abra-ham. Once as Canaan and once as Ham the father of Canaan. Protestant Elizabeth, who finds her opposite as Rome in Catholic Mary, was a negro-trader. God moved the law into the land of the South in which every tribe held Ham as a servant of tribute, and this is the land he chooses with which to demonstrate his laws. Everyone of the seven judges from this South land, of both law and gospel, were slave-holders. Every one of these, except Washington, who stands as Joshua, are not only civil judges, but they also bear the names of the apostles. Not one of which is by accident. These stand for both law and gospel, the same as did David, upon whom God's dual laws met. The only Southern bishop in the church which God has selected as the bride to the husband, and who was chosen to the office because he was a non-slaveholder, God made a slaveholder. With this array of facts in confirming the truth of God, "Canaan shall serve Japheth," men are halting and slumbling the same as did the doubting Thomas. If nothing less than the putting the finger in the prints of the nails will satisfy them, they will have that before it is done. Will Ham be again restored to his normal position as a servant of tribute? This is equivalent to asking, will God's dead witnesses, as Moses and Christ, or civil law and soul law, stand upon their feet again? For what purpose did God give man a law if he intended him to follow the law of his nature? All men have souls, and are subjects to the laws' action. As Ham is mentally too weak to come to the laws of God of himself, God has forced it upon Shem and Japheth to bring him to it, that all may be one in Christ, not one in Moses.

What says God's types upon the restoration of Ham as a servant of tribute? Sarah, the law of gospel, was captured twice from Abraham—once by Egypt, and once by Abimilech. This Abimilech is the same as the seventh judge of Israel, bearing the name of Abimilech. Rebecca, the church of gospel, the wife of Isaac, was also captured by Abimilech. This Rebecca has no existence in gospel Israel till all the symbols for her to arise are filled. Thus must be after the captivity of the woman, or word of God, for 1260 years, and also after one arises and goes into the land of "Red Esau," and then recrosses the ocean, as did Jacob the brook, to wrestle with the angel. Abimilech came at the end of the seventh judge of this Israel from the North, as James Buchanan, and has captured both Sarah and Rebecca. When he restored Rebecca, it was with all the men and maid servants, and a thousand pieces of silver. Why did Abimilech restore Rebecca to Isaac? He saw Isaac sporting with her and took her to be his wife. When this Abimilech sees that God has chosen the husband and bride, in this land, by his own types and his own laws, he will then learn for what purpose God has stirred up the nation to act as it has done, and all hands will feel better. The captivity of the Israel of Shem, by Antiochas Epiphines, for three years and a half after the second building of the temple, was a double symbol of the captivity of gospel Israel. This captivity symbolized the forty-two months, that gospel Israel was in captivity to "mystical Babylon," in Europe, and counts a day for a year, or twelve hundred and sixty years. The captivity of gospel Israel in the land of Japheth's enlargement is for forty-two months or twelve hundred and sixty days, or for three days and a half. In the first as gospel the word or laws of God were in captivity, and Luther found her chained to a block, and he and his coadjutors released her. The second captivity is for the component bodies as organized under the teachings of that word. These are civil law and church law. They come each as the seventh with the heads of both out of the tribe of Judah, or from "between his feet," by the most exact demonstration of truth the world has ever seen.

The question does not stop here. What says the law of Moses in reference to the jubilee, "Thou shalt number seven Sabbaths of years unto thee, seven times seven years, and the space of the seven Sabbaths of years shall be unto thee forty and nine years." Then shalt thou cause the trumpet of the jubilee to sound throughout all your land, and you shall hallow the fiftieth year and every one shall return to his possession. The seven times seven heads of civil governments have brought up the jubilee when universal liberty is proclaimed throughout the land; all in exact agreement with the types as set in literal Israel.

Moses proceeds in this same connection to give further directions. After speaking of the children of Israel as God's servants: "Both thy bond-men and bond-maids shall be of the heathen round about you, and ye shall take them for an inheritance for you and your children forever." These bond-men, to the Israel of Shem that set the type, were the Canaanites, in the land of Canaan. In the anti-type given to Japheth, they were to be the "merchandise of Ethiopia;" in reference to Shem and Japheth they were to be the heathen round about you. Shem and Japheth are Asia and Europe, and the heathen round about these was Ham or Africa—these Shem and Japheth shall inherit forever. Ham is to be a "hewer of wood and a drawer of water," according to the law of Joshua, "unto this day," or "according unto the last day."

The sounding of the jubilee, at the end of the forty-nine heads of civil law, is the announcement to the world that the jubilee of God has come, in which his witnesses shall put off their sack-cloth. It is to tell to the world that he is going to renew the broken tables that holds his laws, and that the "rod of Moses is going to swallow up" all the rods of the world's Egypt, and that he is going to "beat the sword into plough shears and pruning hooks, and that while Shem and Japheth are to teach Ham in spiritual matters, they are to make him hold these plough shears and pruning hooks six days in seven, and they are to "circumcise him," as did Abra-Ham by making him conform to God's law of the flesh.

It might be claimed, with a fair show of reason, that God has used Ham in the relation of a servant for a demonstrative purpose; first, as a type in Canaan to the Israel of Shem, and, secondly, as the anti-type to the Israel of Japheth in the land of his enlargement over Shem; and having used him for this single purpose of knowing in what lands were to look for the Israel to whom the laws were given, and the Israel in which they were fulfilled, the time for Ham to be used as a servant of tribute is up, and he must now go free. As the question is one of great importance, it deserves to be considered in all its bearings We do not regret that Ariel has written his little work on Ham, with all the injustice he has done him. Without the least respect to the plurality of God's creatures of man, in which they may have been one for every continent; they are all made of one blood, and the subjects of the same laws, and are all in the image of God. This oneness is the unity to which they shall come in the "last days." This unity is the justification by faith in the son of God, and is a spiritual unity. There are no steps to this altar, while in a civil sense they will all be the subjects of the laws of Moses.

The six days to make the world are prophetic days of future things, and may have no respect to that which preceded in reference to the literal creation. They stand as prophetic of that that was to be. This being a demonstrated truth, it remains among God's secret things, in reference to how much respect they may have to the literal creation. These six days were God's measured times to give this world to his son, or the laws of his son as the "second Adam;" the same truth may apply to Shem, Ham and Japheth. These may have had a unity of origin, or they may have had a plurality of origin; yet whether the one or the other, whether the one was made in Europe and the other is Asia, and the other in Africa, the purpose of God is that they shall all come together in unity, because all are made in his image. Science need not study to contradict the revealed word of God, for that is an impossibility; science may study to learn man how to read that word correctly. God never leaves himself without a witness. Ham was used as the symbol of the man that would be found in Africa in "the last days." He is used in the same sense that "Red Esau" was used to represent the American Indian. As for whether the one or the other was in literal fact the literal projenitor of the other, are matters of idle speculation. Isaac is "The Christ," that is, he stands to represent "the Christ;" he is used in the same sense that Ham is used to represent Africa. Man would act with the same reason that would go and dig up the grave of Isaac and look for the wound in his side and the nails in his hands, as to go to the Mummies of Egypt and look for the forms and moulds and hairs of the present Ham, in the literal descendants of the first man, Ham. A prophetic action of a future event need be no more a literal fact than the parables of the New Testament are literal facts. When God could swear by no other he sware by himself. When there is no predicate, God makes a predicate. If a father had two sons, an "elder and a younger," God is that father. The Israel's of law and gospel, are the two sons. In this parabolic sense, the characters of Genesis, who preceded Moses, may stand for assumed characters to represent things to be, or they may have been literal characters. That all that is said of them is not literal, is a truth. How much is literal and how much is assumed, is among God's secret things, and are not a matter of practical concern with this generation. That which concerns men now is, are the literal facts in these "last days," such as God said they would be in, in the "last days." If Ham in the "last days" was to be released from being a "servant of tribute," Jacob makes no mention of it in blessing the tribe of Issachar, but confirms it for the last days, "He bowed his shoulder to bear, and became a servant of tribute." This would indicate that the time for this service to begin had just began. If God has kept Ham for a demonstrative purpose only, upon the same reasoning all the principles of laws, taught by all these tribes, may have been brought forward for a demonstrative purpose. Every tribe of Rachel's teaching is a tribe of perpetuity. Once, only, is Jacob the husband of Leah; Jacob is the "Holy Ghost." This is at the tribe of Isaac-er, the servant of tribute. All the other tribes of Leah, except Judah, that gives the national name are demonstrative tribes, and that for which they have been used as the ceremonial law, and forcible law, and the law of division and equilibrium, &c., will pass away. Not so with the teaching of the tribe of Isaac-er. He is a tribe of perpetuity. Would God require six thousand years to demonstrate the meaning of his laws, that make the "tree of knowledge," and then desert them after having thus demonstrated their sense? Would God make Rachel bring forth Joseph as the church, and select that sect from among the seven as the bride, that places the greatest stress upon the doctrine for the soul, "Ye must be born again," and which makes that paramount to any outward law, and then desert his own demonstrated truth? Will God take the tribe of Benjamin, standing for the law of Moses, and after demonstrating that, as his law, cease to use it for the purpose had in view, all the while the demonstration has been going on? If Dan, as the tribe of Rachel, teaches, "the voice of the people in their tribe capacity is the voice of God," will it cease to be the law after the demonstration is finished? If the tribe of Isaac-er is given to represent Ham, begotten, not by the will of the flesh, but by "the Holy Ghost," and in spite of the law of the flesh, will the service end after the truth is demonstrated? If two hundred years with Ham, in his normal relation, as a servant, has raised him so far above the beast in this Israel, as to set up the claim of his equality with Japheth, how many years would it require of Shem and Japheth, to take the whole of Ham from his native land, and elevate him to his normal position as an immortal being possessed of a soul, and subject to the laws of God? Can Ham ever learn these great truths in his native land? All nations of Shem and Japheth, excel all others in some respects of either art or science. In what does Ham excel? In the very same in which he excelled in the second test with his father Noah, in stupidity and ignorance. "The latter days," finds him the world's ass, just as Jacob said of him at the first—he is not a white ass, but a black ass.

When Deborah sings of Israel's victory, she says, "Speak ye that ride on white asses, (white servants,) ye that sit in judgment, and walk by the way." Respect is here had to those who would enslave their own brethren and make them servants of tribute, instead of Ham. Deborah is to gospel, or David, as Miriam is to Moses, or law. The song of Deborah is for gospel Israel given to Japheth. Deborah, as gospel, was the nurse of Rebecca, the church of the gospel. That the world is again put on test is the truth. What then is the nature of this test? Is it to see whether Adam and Eve will bring forth the Nahash, or the "sons of God, as Cain and Seth," to overcome the Nahash, at first begotten? This is not the test. Is it to see which of Noah's sons will follow the "Nahash," as Ham, and which God will choose to overcome him, as Shem and Japheth? This is not the nature of the test. Is it again to bring forth a written law as that which was brought forth at the close of the law given to Shem, when the laws met on the person of "the Christ?" Is it to bring forth the nation of civil law, as the United States, which came at the close of law given to Japheth, in Europe, or the seven churches, that also came from Europe, as the bride to the husband? This is not it. What then is the object of the test? It is to show what is meant by civil law, as taught in the book, that came at the close of Shem, and also what is meant by soul law as taught in the same book. All outside of these are the "Nahash," or they are Hammen, because they follow the laws of nature, as did Ham. Who makes the selection? God himself makes it. Is one party to be praised or blamed more than the other in the selection? No more than was Saul of Tarsus, when he was a persecutor of God's people. Do these facts have anything to do in reference to the salvation of the parties in heaven? Not a word of it. They are chosen as God's demonstrative parties, which sit in judgment upon action in this life. The future life is tried upon motives. God has granted to none the right to sit in judgment upon his fellows in reference to the future life. A moral inability to keep the law rests upon all men, until God demonstrates its meaning. "God is not a hard master." "He remembereth we are dust." Men will fight, and kill, and steal, and think they are doing God service, until God teaches his own meaning to these prohibitions. All Ham men are those who follow the law of nature, as did Ham. God himself designates the heads of these in this land. They are Abra-Ham and Ham-lin. Those who represent the civil law, as at first set up, are Jefferson and A. Hambleton Stevens, as the corresponding opposites to the Ham-man. Is this done out of spite to his creatures? No; it is for their instruction and enlightenment. A knowledge of this truth to this Ham-man may lead him to build his gallows higher and increase the bonds of Israel—no matter. He cannot bind the word of God, nor can he go beyond God's prescribed limits; "No power can be given him except it were from above." The king will open the book at the right time and inquire for the conspirators to take his life. The word of the king is the life of the king. His honor is pledged that it shall not fail. If Joseph has his feet in fetters, it does not matter, or if Daniel is in the den, the king will be there, or if Herod beheads John, it is because his work is done. God set the types and he will see that they are every one fulfilled. This is his own method to lift the scales from the eyes of "Saul of Tarsus." The world is fighting the battle of Ham-man-gog, standing to oppose the laws of God.—See Ezekiel 39th chap.

We take leave of the tribe of Issachar, the servant of tribute, and shall find what God requires of Judah concerning him, when he sums up the tribes. In the blessing of Moses upon this tribe, he unites him with Zebulon, which will be considered in connection with Zebulon.

At the birth of the tribe of Zebulon, Leah said, "Now will my husband dwell with me because I have born him six sons." It was at the birth of the tribe of Zebulon that Leah took possession of the civil government, as the husband. The tribe of Zebulon in this land is Florida. This tribe came in Israel in the year 1821. This was the year in which this land, as the Israel of law, divided the husband as the civil government. The tribe of Benjamin, or Texas, was cast out at the same time that Leah took possession of the husband. Benjamin was given in exchange for Florida, in the negotiations with Spain for Florida. As the law of unity in Israel, for which Benjamin stood, was cast out by the division of Israel, so moves the tribe of Benjamin. As Leah had brought forth the Israel of law, closing with the tribe of Judah, so she had to bring forth the nation of Judah, in which all the tribes were to be located. This act of Leah in taking the husband, was that Israel might journey forty years in the wilderness for the second settlement of Israel, the same as Israel had journeyed forty years from the tribe of Judah for the first settlement. The act which gave Leah the husband was in violation of the law upon which Israel had been set up. Both Reuben and Simeon, or Virginia, and Plymouth, had said the law of Israel was "States rights," and that "Governments were by consent of the governed." Neither of these were respected in the act of bringing Zebulon. The law was doubly violated in that the inhabitants of Zebulon were not consulted in respect to whether they would become a tribe in Israel, nor was Benjamin consulted in respect to whether he would be exchanged for Zebulon. God intended by this act to show to Israel that while his law is that of "States rights," it is not by the "consent of the governed."

Israel may consent to choose a king, or any other law, than that of God, and it will always be under God's "solemn protest." This doctrine, in this Israel, has reversed the order of God, and instead of holding "Ham as a servant of tribute," it has made Japheth to become the servant of tribute. It is only Simeon making Reuben drink the dregs of his own folly, in this land of Japheth's enlargement, the same that Simeon in Rome has done to Reuben, as the Israel of law from Shem. For forty and two months, or 1260 years, has Simeon, as the second son, joined with Levi, made Reuben, as the first born, or Israel of law, pay bitterly for teaching the doctrine that "governments are by consent." For forty and two months, or 1260 days in this Japhetic Israel, will Simeon, as the second son, or Plymouth, in connection with Levi, as the church, make Reuben as the first, or Virginia, pay dearly for teaching the doctrine that "governments are by the consent of the governed. When God has used Simeon as the second son, whether in the person of the Pope of Rome, in whom the gospel of Judah was changed to the "man of sin," or, as the Puritan Cromwell, that made the second foot of Judah to represent Simeon, or whether as the Methodist Episcopal Church in the North of this Japhetic Israel, that dates from gospel Judah, his ministers of vengeance to drive his elect Israel to demonstrate his truth; the agent thus used will become as Babylon, both in reference to "mystical Babylon," and the Virgin daughter of Babylon."

The taking of the husband by Leah at the coming of Zebulon was the announcement made, that Israel had began the second journey in the wilderness. This was at the coming of the half tribe Ephraim in 1821, which was the first tribe of Israel to cross over the Jordan. As Manassah, or Kentucky, was the first to come to the original, or first Israel, so the other son of Joseph, as Ephraim, begins the second journey for the second half. If seventy years be determined upon Israel from the first, as Manassah, or from 1791 to 1861, it counts forty years from the second, or from 1821 to 1861. It is Leah that divides Israel. Rachel never divides. Leah divides to demonstrate what Rachel teaches. When it is finished, Rachel will take the world. Leah divided Israel at the coming of Zebulon, in 1821. In blessing Zebulon, Jacob said, "Zebulon shall dwell at the haven of the sea, and shall be an haven for ships, and his border shall be unto Zidon." This is the only tribe in Israel that every part of which borders the sea, and he represents the commerce of the Japhetic Israel; and as he is the chosen tribe to represent the whole of that commerce, his border shall be to the Northern extremity of Israel, as was the literal Zidon. This account, perhaps, is a thousand years older than Zidon. It is a prophecy belonging to the Japhetic Israel, yet resting upon the Israel of Shem for its typical character, though much older than Zidon in the land of Shem. When Moses came to bless the tribes, he united the two tribes, Zebulon and Issachar, saying, "Rejoice Zebulon, in thy going out, and Issachar in thy tents. They shall call the people unto the mountain, there shall they offer the sacrifices of righteousness, for they shall suck of the abundance of the seas, and of treasures hid in the sand."

The two tribes of Simeon and Levi, united by Jacob, are given to show church and State union, so the two united by Moses in the land of Japheth's enlargement, are given to point out both the civil law and soul law of God.

Forty years from the coming of Issachar, in 1803–4, and the the church of gospel was cut off by the division of the Methodist church, in this land, in 1844. Forty years from the tribe of Zebulon, in 1821, and the civil law was put up in Naphtali, the place of Rachel's triumph. If to the difference of one hundred years, as the difference of the double times for cleansing the sanctuary, as 2300 years and 2400 years, Sabbatic days be added, it is equal to fourteen years; if this fourteen be added to 1844, it is equal to 1858. This was the time that the church ordered all condemnation of slavery to be left out of the book of law. If two jubilee years be added to the one hundred, according to the law of Moses, it is two years, this would make 1860. It was the year following this that "Rachel prevailed" in both civil law and soul law. These counts are from the heads that stand as moon and sun. Spain is the moon, Florida is Spain; France is the sun, Louisiana is France; England is the earth. This ended with Georgia, for the first count of forty years for both law and gospel at Philadelphia

The same law and the same sect for the church of gospel that were first set up at the end of forty years at Philadelphia from "the earth that conbines both sun and moon," are the same in the second settlement. As in the literal Israel, the forerunner John, brought the Apostle Andrew, the first apostle, to Christ, that stood for the apostles, as the seventh head for gospel, or the law of the soul; so at the end of 2300 years, for the first cleansing of the sanctuary, the Rev. John Wesley organized his church in London, upon the principle that "laymen were not to take down the ark nor set it up." At the end of 2400 years for the second cleansing of the sanctuary, that church which Wesley set up in this land, was the second time cleansed by bringing Andrew, in the person of the Rev. Bishop Andrew, as the head of the seventh sect, or gospel church, out of the tribe of Judah, as the tribe that gave him birth, and also out of the tribe of Levi, as he was a member of the South Carolina Conference, in order to show the one was transferred to the other, the same as Christ, in the person of Matthew, whose name was Levi, was transferred to the gospel in Judah. There is in these types and their fulfillment the most exact yet complicated arrangements of facts the world has ever known. Nothing but the God that made the world could have done it: "I go where no man's building is." He will allow no imposter to intrude upon his demonstration of both the husband and the bride.

"Rejoice Zebulon in thy going out." Zebulon is the only tribe that makes a horn in the sea in his going out."

and Issachar in thy tents, and it might be added in thy coming in. If the one, as a horn, goes into the sea, the sea runs into the other, and as the labor of Issachar living in his tents, finds ingress and egress through Issachar, it is only an enlargement of the idea as at first expressed in reference to the river that parted into four heads, in which one head as the Gihon "compassed the whole land of Ethiopia." These tribes shall call the people to the mountain," being the two of Leah, after she commenced bearing the second time, from which to date God's forms of civil and soul laws, the truth which they demonstrate will call the people to the mountain of the Lord's house, which are his laws and which are Jerusalem. "They shall gather treasures hid in the sand." The literal Moses killed an Egyptian and hid him in the sand. This act was symbolic of how the laws of God would kill every Egyptian law. Moses was gone after this act for forty years, and returned with his wife Zipporah—so with the laws of God; gone forty years from the coming of the tribe of Zebulon, that law returns to national Judah, and it tells who the bride is to the husband, and explains the symbol of the literal Moses in hiding the Egyptian in the sand. These are the only tribes that give meaning to the act of Moses. As moves the literal characters to set the types in Shem, so moves the laws for which the literal stands in the Israel of Japheth.

The six tribes of Leah and the four of the two maid servants, have now been considered. They have been considered according to the order of their birth, and not the order of their blessing. What a pleasure it would have been to such a mind as the good and learned Dr. A. Clark, could he have looked upon these tribes in their physical locality, and found every perplexing question answered for him. He seemed troubled to know why the tribe of Issachar, which came before Zebulon in the order of birth, should be preceded by Zebulon in drawing his lot and receiving his blessing. The six of Leah, all border the coast, and when Jacob begins with Reuben to bless, he takes them in the regular order of physical locality, stepping from Judah to Zebulon, and closing with Issachar. This arrangement places Zebulon before Issachar with his lot and blessing, though in point of fact Issachar, is before Zebulon. The same fact applies to the four servants—Jacob begins with Dan, then Gad, then Asher, and ends with Naphtali, as the place of setting up the civil government. We cannot dwell here, and only aim to suggest to the reflective world what a treasure it has in the "Book of God"—the only book. How small a portion of the book is yet learned!

After these ten tribes were born, Rachel prayed to God, and she says, "The Lord hath heard my petition," and she bear a son and called his name Joseph; this is the child of prayer; to him the birthright is given, and he has no inheritance but a double portion. The double laws, for which Abraham stood, and which were confirmed in Isaac and in Jacob, were given to Joseph, and they closed in the two sons of Joseph. It is the bones of Joseph that have to be brought out of Egypt. Joseph is the same as David. If Joseph is the seventh type of Christ, David is the seventh son of Jesse. Joseph is the civil law of God, as given in the days of judges, and the soul law as given in the days of apostles. These make the birth-right of God.

At the birth of Joseph, Jacob said, "Send me away to my country and to my place." In the Israel of Shem, Levi, as the church, had no inheritance. Levi was joined with Simeon in gospel Israel, given to Japheth. When Israel is sent away to his place in the land of Japheth's enlargement, Levi stood for all the scattered churches. In this demonstrative Israel, when the birthright is given to Joseph, Levi has an inheritance.

The two tribes of Rachel, as Benjamin and Joseph, are the summaries of laws to the other ten tribes. These are "Moses and Christ." These laws of God are sent in mercy to the world to save it from wars and contentions, the same as Joseph was sent to his brethren upon an errand of mercy. As the brethren of Joseph treated him badly, saying, "Shall this dreamer rule over us," so have the laws of God been treated badly in this world. Man has followed the laws of nature, saying, "Shall this dreamer rule over us." If the one says, "Thou shalt not kill," nor "Covert thy neighbors servant," man has found out a better way to serve God than by following his direction. If the other says, "Ye must be born again," man has found out some other way to climb up and follow the laws of nature, with saying, "How can these things be?" This Joseph, like the laws for which he stands, must prophecy in sackcloth and ashes his appointed time. As Joseph is the summary of both the civil law of Judah and the church, and the same characters in him fill up either in this land, we will leave him for the present, with remarking that he was sent away the second time to his people and country, in the year 1844, at the division of the Methodist Episcopal Church, in this land. At his birth, Rachel said, "The Lord shall add to me another son." This other son is Benjamin, and is Texas, of whom we have already spoken somewhat, and will aim to be brief. At the birth of Benjamin, Rachel died. Benjamin came in this land in 1845, and the word of God, for the government of Israel died. As the law of Benjamin retired from the North and still prevailed in the South from the passage of the Missouri Compromise line, so the tribe of Benjamin moves in Israel. Reuben and Simeon, J. Monroe and J. Q. Adams, cast out Benjamin and Reuben, and Levi, or J. Tyler and J. C. Calhoun, brought him back. Benjamin was the tribe that had the cup in his sack. The steward said in respect to this cup, "This is it by which my Lord divineth," that is, the law of Moses is that by which God judgeth. Law, as Abraham, had gone through this land, from the Atlantic to the Pacific ocean, and closed under the last of the seven Southern judges, as James K. Polk. The tribe of Benjamin, the son of Rachel, was allowed to gain his independence to show to Israel how a foreign nation should come to Israel. "Cast lots for him," is not only the divine method in making an apostle, but also in admitting a tribe to join Israel. These lots are to be cast as tribes holding the law of Moses, that is, if not legislating to make Ham a servant of tribute, they are forbid any impediment in rendering him back to his rightful owner The "Wilmot Proviso" of 1847, was the death of Rachel, as the law of God. Then it was that "five kings served four twelve years, and in the thirteenth year they rebelled, and in the fourteenth they went to war, (as recorded in the book of Genesis,) and the four whipped the five." These kings are the world's four lawgivers. The Israel of law, from Shem, said it was all Moses, and these represent Levi. The Israel of gospel, in Rome, said it was Simeon and Levi, united by the will of man. That the Pope held the keys of Peter, and he could loose and bind, that is, it was all Judah or gospel. The Israel of law in this land of Japheth, said it was "Governments are by consent of the governed," and "Religion was free." Finding this would not answer they said, the thing needed was to divide Israel in both civil and soul laws. These four kings are common to both wings of Israel—the South had one other king, and said, commerce or cotton was king. Five of these served four from 1847, twelve years, to 1859 ; in the thirteenth year they rebelled," and Levi, or South Carolina, withdrew, and in the fourteenth year, or in 1861, they went to war. Abraham, or law, armed his own trained servants, born in his house, (318,) and brought back all the goods and victuals that had been captured by the four. (The number 318 has respect to the whole electorial college in this land.) Three young men confederated with Abraham These are, Executive, Legislative and Judicial. The arming of Ham, with the ballot, was contrary both to the law of Abraham and also of Judah, whom it will be seen "binds his own foal to the vine," or civil law, with his asses colt to the choice vine, as Joseph the church. The restoration of law will show the illegality of the act of putting the ballot in the hands of the servant, and thus all things will be restored by using him as the agent. The king of Sodom, one of the same kings that had been slain by the four, met Abraham coming from the slaughter, which shows though the land be a very Sodom in wickedness, it is still the land of God's selection in which to demonstrate his laws to man. Let none pride themselves upon their own goodness or righteousness, because God as a sovereign act has chosen the land in which to set up his laws. Jacob said of Benjamin, "Benjamin shall raven as a wolf; in the morning he shall devour the prey, and in the evening he shall divide the spoil." Moses said of Benjamin, "The beloved of the Lord shall dwell in safety by him, and the Lord shall cover him all the day long, and he shall dwell between his shoulders." These blessings have respect both to the law of Moses, for which Benjamin stands, and the Israel of law to whom the law was given. "In the morning he shall raven as a wolf." Benjamin is one of the witnesses that turns water to blood as often as he will. Wars are the result of man's disobedience to the law of God for which Benjamin stands. The law may be driven about the same as the nation to whom it was given, yet in the evening both shall be brought in. The Lord will take care of both, as both will be required to complete the "fullness of the Gentiles." These, as Benjamin, are the burning bush of Moses—forever burning, yet never destroyed. Benjamin dwells between the shoulders, in the same sense that the law-giver comes from between the feet of Judah. While Reuben says, "If I bring not Benjamin, slay my two sons." It is national Judah that says, "Take me and put me in prison for the sake of Benjamin." Unless God had taken this nation of Judah and imprisoned him and brought him along at every step, just as he has, it was not possible for men by human wisdom to understand those symbols for which they stand. While the tragedy is a terrible one, and the heart-rending anguish is indescribable, yet the happy results to grow therefrom, will through a thousand years of peace and quiet, more than recompense for all this suffering. These judgments fall with terrible weight upon the generations whom God selects to enlighten the world. Yet God is good, and he commands sun and moon to "stand still," and thus he suspends the rigid exactions of his own laws, and in the end it may be that none shall claim advantage over the others.

Each tribe in Israel demands a separate chapter, to be considered in the full sense of that they are given to teach. We leave Benjamin to see what is taught by the two half tribes of Joseph as "Manassah and Ephraim," or Kentucky and Missouri. These are half tribes because they divide between civil law and soul law. Their mother was an Egyptian woman, and the laws for which they stand are what God has brought out of the dragon of the world's Egypt, or the Beast of Babylon. They stand to represent the double portion given to Joseph. If Manassah is law, Ephraim is both law and gospel. The dream of Joseph had respect to the division of this Japhetic Israel in both a civil and gospel sense. "The first is last, and the last is first." Joseph dreamed that the sheaf of his brethren bowed to his sheaf. This is political, and stands for the eleven tribes that bowed to him in the Southern Confederacy. He dreamed again, and the "eleven stars, sun and moon bowed to him." This is the division of the church of gospel, when not only the eleven but the two, as Manassah and Ephraim, standing as "sun and moon," bowed down to Joseph. Jacob interpreted this dream to Joseph, will "I and your mother, and your brethren bow down to you?" "I and your mother" stand as sun and moon; she is the moon that holds the written law, and I am the sun as "God the Holy Ghost," to give the spirit to the law.

This dream was never literally fulfilled in literal Israel; Rachel never went down to Joseph in Egypt, hence she never "bowed to him." Jacob tells the sense when he comes to bless the sons of Joseph, "Let my name and the names of my fathers, Abraham and Isaac, rest upon the lads." As these heads of laws stood for "sun and moon," so the half tribes of Joseph would stand for "sun and moon." The moon is law, the sun is gospel. Jacob said, "These are mine, as Reuben and Simeon, they shall be mine." "The issue that thou begettest after these shall be them." Reuben and Simeon have stood for laws in all of the history of Israel. Thus it is with the two sons of Joseph; they are "sun and moon," or law and gospel. The first born of Joseph was Manassah, and is the half tribe of Kentucky; the second is Ephraim, and is Missouri. At the birth of Manassah, Joseph said, "The Lord hath made me forget all my toil, and all of my father's house." At the birth of Ephraim, Joseph said, "The Lord hath caused me to be fruitful in the land of my affliction."

The half tribe Manassah was on the East of the Jordan, in the Israel of Shem, and Ephraim was on the West, as in the Israel of Japheth, yet the order of the other tribes is reversed. The journeyings of God's Israel will find no rest until it reaches the symbols of the two half tribes of Joseph, as moon and sun, or law and gospel. The brethren of Joseph standing for human kings, in opposition to the laws of God, as the king returned to Jacob with the coat of many colors, all stained with blood, and Jacob mourned for him as dead. These were symbols of "the Christ," upon whom the laws of God met, and also of the nation of the Christ, in which the same laws were to meet. If Joseph was put in prison, the Christ was laid in the sepulchre of Joseph, standing for his prison, and the nation taking the laws is in prison. If a guard over him in the one case was required, so is the other. If the tribe of Manassah, representing the first half of Israel, in this land of Japheth, is law, as the first tribes to come to the original tribes, so is the half tribe Ephraim the first tribe to represent the second half of Israel, across the Jordan, and he stands for both law and gospel. If the rebuilding of Jerusalem counts seventy years for the captivity from Manassah to 1861, or from 1791 to 1861, it counts forty years for Israel to journey in the wilderness from Ephraim, or from 1821 to 1861. These are half tribes, whether the count is from East to West, or from North to South. The half tribe to divide Israel is Manassah; the half tribe to unite Israel is Ephraim. If the two kings to divide Israel, as Saul and David, or Abraham Lincoln and Jefferson Davis, were both born in Manassah, it is the same tribe to which the church goes to complete its division in Louisville in 1845. All the tribes of Israel, like the apostles, move by pairs as half tribes. Two are law-givers, as Levi and Judah; two show the laws departures, as Reuben and Simeon; two are given as the flying wings of the cherubim, these are Issachar and Zebulon, the four as servants, are two of Rachel and two of Leah; two are summaries of law, as Joseph and Benjamin; two are given to show the place of Israel's rest, as Manassah and Ephraim. Ephraim is the tribe to bring the world back to the starting point; in him dwelt the first Adam that lost a world; in him will go the world's Rome, to claim the world by the second Adam; Cain cast out built a city that divided Israel—this was Constantine and Constantinople. Fourteen generations from this time, and the law of Cain was restored in Lamech. The city builded was in honor of the first judge, as Washington, and Washington City. Fourteen generations from this first judge finds Israel in captivity with the law-giver from "between the feet of Judah." This law-giver bears the name of the second Southern judge of the Southern wing of Israel, that stands for the second half of Israel beyond the

Jordan; his name is Jefferson. It is said of Manassah that he shall represent his thousands, while of Ephraim, he shall represent his "ten thousands," and shall become "mu'ti- tudes of nations." These facts would seem to indicate that the name of the city in Ephraim, bearing the names both of the judge of the second half of Israel, and also the law- giver from "between the feet of Judah," was God's chosen place for the world's Rome. We would not speculate in these thoughts, but write suggestively. Do you understand?

While from the half tribe, Manassah, the laws must count that build Jerusalem, it is into the half tribe, Ephraim, that the seat of the laws thus demonstrated, will be located. These laws will heal the nations, as the leaves of the trees that grow upon either bank of the river. They stand as the literal demonstrated book of God, as body and soul civil law, and soul law, Old and New Testament, Moses and Christ, Levi and Judah, Benjamin and Joseph, Manassah and Ephraim, the civil government of the Southern Con- federacy, and the church government of the Methodist Episcopal Church, South.

Does the reader say, "I can't believe it!" God's types all say you would not. You were not to know it. The Queen Esther, that Ahasuerus selected, was the only one under trial that followed the exact directions of the king's steward; hence she was the one chosen as the bride to the king. The laws of God are the king. These laws are so interpreted by the types and God's fulfillment, in the histo- ry given of their exposition, God has determined you shall believe before it is done. "The watchmen shall come to see eye to eye."

The half tribe of Manassah is law, and stands to Ephraim, in this demonstrated Israel, as Benjamin to Judah; the laws for which these stand are Jerusalem. The seventy weeks of Daniel to the coming of the prince, upon whom the laws met, are in this land seventy years. Seven weeks are seven times, or seven years, as the seven times seven heads of civil law, are seven times, or simply seven years, as in the case of Nebuchadnezzar. A week is a time, but a time is a year, it follows from hence that a week is a year. In reference to these measures, it depends upon what sym- bol is followed. A month is also a year in this land of the literal. The seven months that the Ark of Noah was float- ing upon the waters, are the same in value as the "seven times that passed over Nebuchadnezzar."

This seven times were only seven years, and covered both ends of the indignation, the last end was for forty-two months. In this land of the literal, both ends are for eighty-four years, or from 1776 to 1860–1. All the former symbols of Israel, which have been given by the movements and cycles of the celestial heavens, are in this governed by the cycles of the literal earth and sun; seventy weeks are seventy years.

With this explanation, let us read the prophecy of Daniel concerning the rebuilding of Jerusalem, that is the laws for which Jerusalem stood, which in the person of Messiah, became the substitutes for the literal house. "Seventy years are determined upon thy people," and upon the laws for which Jerusalem stood as the holy city. The bringing in of these laws will finish the transgression in a national sense, and make an end of sins, and will make reconciliation for iniquity, and will bring in the laws of God, as the everlasting righteousness, and unseal the vision and prophecy, and annoint the Most Holy.

Know therefore and understand that from the going forth of the commandment to restore and build Jerusalem, unto the coming of the laws of the Prince, there shall be seven years, and three score years, and two years. The laws of Jerusalem come will together again in times of great trouble and after three score and two years, the component bodies that are chosen to represent the same laws, that met on Messiah, shall be cut off, but not for their own transgressions, and the people of the invading prince shall destroy the laws that make Jerusalem and the sanctuary, and desolations are determined upon to the end of the week, or seven years, which Jacob will serve to get Rachel. And the invading prince shall confirm the covenant with many for one week, or seven years, and in the midst of the week he shall cause the sacrifice and the oblation to cease, by putting up a human God in the stead of the laws of God, and to the end of the war desolations are determined upon.

The reading of this mysterious prophecy in Daniel has been praphrased to make it conform to the literal facts in the Japhetic Israel given to "unseal the book." This prophecy is given to show the double signification to be applied to Jerusalem. Seventy weeks are required to overthrow the literal Jerusalem, and to substitute the laws that met upon the literal house, upon the person of the Messiah, that became the substitute of the literal house. This prophecy had respect to the literal Israel as a type, but to the Japhetic Israel in a more particular and exact sense. We have never seen any expositor that could make the prophecy apply in all its parts to the literal coming of Christ, and the literal overthrow of Jerusalem. Two things are to be done at one and the same time—Jerusalem is to be overthrown, and yet in the overthrow the transgression is to be finished, and an end of sins is to come, &c. The laws for which Jerusalem stood are Benjamin and Judah, or Joseph. These are Moses and Christ, or civil law and soul law. When these unite, according to the types, there is an end of sin, and transgressions are finished. As these united on "the Christ," so are they to unite in the nation given to Japheth, that was to bring forth the fruits of the kingdom. If, after they unite, they are not overthrown by the invading prince, the prophecy is not fulfilled. If the invading prince does not confirm the covenant for one week that existed between Benjamin as law, and Judah as gospel, for one week or seven years, the prophecy is not fulfilled. If, in the midst of that week, the laws that represent Jerusalem, or the Messiah, are not cut off, the prophecy is not fulfilled. Let us now look at a few of the leading particulars as they apply to the literal facts of this Japhetic Israel, substituting one single form of civil law of the seven in the history of Israel, and one church as the soul law of the seven, for the bride to the husband, as soul to body, are gospel to law. As in the first setling of Israel, forty years from the tribe of Judah, the civil and church blend together as body and soul, so they must blend together in reading this prophecy. The half tribe Manassah stands in this Israel as law, and it is the first tribe that came to the original twelve, and is the proper tribe to date the rebuilding of the gospel Jerusalem from. "Seventy years are determined upon thy people" from the coming of the halftribe Manassah, or Kentucky, as the tribe from which to date the rebuilding of Jerusalem. This tribe came in the year 1791, seventy years extends to 1861. The order in which this decree will be fulfilled, in setting up both law and gospel, and in making them harmonize so that Abraham, as law, shall cease to disown Sarah, as gospel, is the following:

From the going forth of the decree, for seventy years, as the extreme measures, there shall be seven years to the time when Manassah shall interpret the law for the body, or in the year 1798, he will, by his resolutions, give the interpretation to the civil law that is to build Jerusalem. Three score years from that date, and the church, as the bride, will conform to this civil law of Manassah by blotting out all condemnation of slave-holding. This will be in the year 1858, and is intended to give Moses his Ethiopian bride. Two years from this time, and the two as civil and soul laws will agree together as sixty-nine years, and the year following will complete the seventy that is to overthrow the people that have thus rebuilt Jerusalem between Benjamin and

Judah. This union of the laws, that build Jerusalem, was necessary to annoint David, in his double character, the second time, by Judah alone, as the heads of these laws are both out of the tribe of Judah, in national Judah, the same as the "Christ," upon whom they met, was out of Judah. This annointing of David, by Judah alone, made it necessary for national Judah to separate from national Benjamin, or David from Saul, and in the separation the covenant of union was broken, and the invading prince from Benjamin will reinstate for one week or seven years, in the midst of which the laws that make Jerusalem, or David, as God's two witnesses, will be dead three and one half years. Yet as God intends no separation between Benjamin and Judah, but that Judah shall rule the whole land, this death, or this imprisonment of Judah, is necessary in order that he may bring, not only the law of Benjamin, but also the nation of Benjamin in the Israel of Japheth, the same as he did in the Israel of Shem, when the tribe of Benjamin rebelled against the laws of Israel. As in the first case, Judah exterminated all the tribe of Benjamin, except six hundred men and four hundred women, so in the second he will exterminate every thing out of Benjamin, except the ten commandments of the law of Moses, for which he stands expressed by six and four.

There is no part of this prophecy but what will find its easy and natural interpretation by following each symbol, and giving them their proper places in the interpretation. The civil law, as the husband and the church law, as the soul, are blended together at every point, and hold the same relation as body and soul. The protest of God against the division of the Israel of Shem, which was occasioned by a departure from his form of civil law, as given in the seventh head as judges, was a protest not only against Israel's departure from the law of Moses for the body, but also against the law of Levi, or Moses, for the soul. The departure in the one case led to the departure in the other. It was the cause that led Jeroboam to substitute the "golden heifers" of Samaria for the laws of God, as Jerusalem. The protest of the seventh judge, in this Israel, as Andrew Jackson, born of Levi, as Moses, and whose name as Andrew, was given to show that the Israel of both law and gospel, or national Judah, had been separated from national Benjamin, was the protest of God; like the permit in the division of literal Israel, which set the types, it was for a specific purpose, which, when fulfilled, the protest was to be removed. The same facts apply to the church, in its protest, by the half tribe Manassah, in reference to a division of the gospel, or seventh church. This protest was the work of the Rev.

H. B. Bascomb, of Manassah, and is virtually the protest of God, for this Japhetic Israel, according to types set in Shem. These protests, coming from the tribes they do, which tribes, as law-givers, have the same symbolic sense, are notes of attention, that God is only moving forward to demonstrate his laws, and then when that is finished, the whole shall be reunited upon the laws thus demonstrated. The same facts in either case apply to the civil heads, or churches heads. If the Rev. John Wesley, who stands as the forerunner of the gospel church, adopts the language of the literal John, in reference to the gospel church, "He that cometh after me, is preferred before me," for he was before "me," and he stands represented in his first Apostle, Andrew, the same facts apply to the church of John Wesley, in its relation to the church, headed by Bishop Andrew, as the head of the seventh church, that agrees with the Apostle Andrew. This truth applies alike to the seventh judge as Andrew Jackson, born of Levi. John Quincy Adams might say in truth, according to history, "He that cometh after me is preferred before me, for he was before me." That Jackson was the choice of the people of this land, as judge, before John Adams, is the truth, and that he came in after him, is also true. This question does not stop here, nor can we give more than a tithe of that mountain weight of testimony, which God gives of his demonstrated truth. The leading agents, or forerunners, to make the law in this Japhetic Israel, were Thos. Jefferson and Alexander Hambleton. The heads of laws that come from gospel Judah, represent the same in this Irsael. As the characters of the New Testament are the same as those of the old, so the same characters of the first, or Israel of law, in this Israel of Japheth are the same as those of the second, or Israel of both law and gospel.

The first Israel is not only law, but as law it types the second, as both law and gospel. The first bishop of the church of gospel, in this land, was "Francis Asbury." He stood as the forerunner of Bishop Andrew.

In order to make this truth palpable to the minds of men, the forerunner at the trial of Bishop Andrew, to prepare the way for him, was "Francis A. Harding." We need not dwell upon facts so palpable, that such as would dispute them might also dispute that three angles of a triangle were not equal to two right angles, or that two and two were not four. The God that made man and that made the world has determined that his intelligent creature man shall know that he rules in the affairs of men, and that he means to rule by his own laws.

The two half tribes, as sons of Joseph, are the pivot around which this Israel of Japheth revolves, and they are given to hold it both to unity and instruct it in the laws of God. That which God intends to make great always jars heavy at its birth. The world's center is in Ephraim, of whom he is to represent "multitudes of nations." This tribe stood for ten kingdoms in the second half of Isreal, or in the second half, as in Rome, which was broken into ten kingdoms in West Rome; or he stands for the ten old States in the North of the United States. These are Ephraim "joined to idols." The half tribe Ephraim, as Missouri, will find "room and give rest and prosperity to the world, when in him Judah and Ephraim appoints them one head," and that head is Moses for the body, and Christ for the soul. With these general remarks we take leave of the two half tribes, Manassah and Ephraim.

Judah and Joseph remain to be considered. If to Joseph the birthright belongs, Judah is the law-giver. At the birth of Judah, Leah said, "Now will I praise the Lord, and Leah left bearing." Jacob said of Judah, "Thou art he whom thy brethren shall praise; thy fathers shall bow down before thee." "Judah is a lion's whelp, from the prey my son thou art gone up; he stooped down, he crouched as a lion, and as an old lion; who shall rouse him up?" "The sceptre shall not depart from Judah, nor a law-giver from between his feet, until Shiloh come, and unto him shall the gathering of the people be." "Binding his foal unto the vine, and his ass' colt unto the choice vine; he washed his garments in wine, and his clothes in the blood of grapes." "His eyes shall be red with wine, and his teeth white with milk."

Moses said of Judah, "Let his hands be sufficient for him, and be thou a help to him from his enemies." As in the Israel of Shem, several tribes had their literal portion in the tribe of Judah, so in the Israel of Japheth, all the tribes are represented by national Judah, and he is the summary of all the laws for which they stand. The stone of Bohan, the son of Reuben, in the Israel of Shem, set the northern boundary of Judah. Bohan is the one son of Reuben, and is given to represent the one half of Reuben. In the Israel of Shem, Reuben had five sons, or one standing for the whole. In the Israel of Japheth, Reuben has five sons, or one son standing for the whole. The five States are, Ohio, Indiana, Illinois, Wisconsin and Michigan, are the five that came of Reuben. These five are summed up by the one as Bohan, or Kentucky, that sets the stone of Bohan " as the northern boundary of Judah. This tribe of Bohan, or Kentucky, as a half tribe, holds the same relation to Reuben, the first born son of Leah, as to Joseph, the first born of Rachel; he is a half tribe in either case. With the one half as Benjamin, Reuben defiled the law of God by the ordinance of 1787, while, with the other half, as Judah, he is "the strength of might and the excellency of dignity and power." With the one-half, Reuben said, "States Rights," with the other he said consolidation, upon the principle that "governments are by the consent of the governed," without respect to the laws of God for the civil law of man. The two kings to divide Israel, as Saul and David, or Abraham Lincoln or Jefferson Davis, were each born in the tribe of Bohan, or Manassah, or Kentucky, and the one came from between the feet of the tribe of Judah, in national Judah, and the other from between the tribes with which Reuben defiled himself, in national Benjamin. This Benjamin, or Saul, said in the Israel of Shem that he was the "Lord's annointed," and that David should not come to the throne, in the Israel of Shem and Saul, and Absalom, the son of David, kept David seven years and a half from coming to the throne. David stands for God's own laws, and is no individual man; yet, as individuals were given to seal the laws, so they are given to tell which way the laws of God move in the Japhetic Israel. "God's great host came to David" at the expiration of the seven years, that he was driven into a South land, in the Israel of Shem, as the type of the laws of God. It remains to be seen whether "the great host of God will come to the laws of David, in this Japhetic Israel.

Of Judah it is said "Thy father's children shall bow down to thee." Whether this be ceremonial Reuben, or forcible Simeon, or the law-giver, as Levi, or Dan, as the principle of judging his own people, or Gad, as equilibrium; or Asher, as division; or Issachar, as the ass, or servant; or Zebulon, as the tribe to represent the making Shem and Japheth servants of tribute, in the stead of Ham, or Benjamin, as law. All shall bow down to Judah, out of whom came the Christ, upon whom the laws of God met, and out of whom, in this Japhetic Israel, the heads of those laws have come again. The prophecy concerning Judah is a double prophecy. This prophecy has respect not only to the national Judah, but to the tribe of Judah in the national Judah. What was true in the Israel of Shem, is also true in the Israel of Japheth.

The two tribes of Benjamin and Judah, in the Israel of Shem, stood for as much as the whole twelve. While they were two, as the summaries of laws, the ten sons of the literal Benjamin stand for the ten tribes. These are the ten commandments of the law of Moses as God's law to govern man. Wher they are corrupted by human laws, as in Jeroboam, or as the ten kingdoms of West Rome, they are called ten horns, and are "Ephraim joined to idols." The two tribes were in Babylon, and they symbolized the word or written laws of God in "mystical Babylon," while the ten horns, or kingdoms of Judah, in Rome, existed as so many nations, or tribes. The law of Benjamin is unity. " Whoever offendeth in one part is guilty of the whole because it is one law." These two tribes standing for all the tribes in the days of Israel's unity, were called Judah after Israel divided. They stood as national Judah. In this national Judah, it was the tribe of Judah that gave the Christ upon whom the laws met, so in the Israel of Japheth, it must be the tribe of Judah, in national Judah, from whom the representative heads of laws must come. Not only must the heads of laws come from the tribe of Judah in national Judah, but the scepter must depart from national Judah, at the coming of the head of gospel, as the "Shiloh out" of Judah, while at the coming of the civil head, the two as the representatives of the two witnesses of civil law and soul law, must be killed. In this respect the Israel of the land of Japheth's enlargement must fill up the double ending of the Israel of Shem in Judah, and the Israel of gospel, in Europe, given to Japheth. The scepter departed from Judah at the coming of Shiloh, in the Israel of Shem, but their nationality did not at that time depart. In the middle of the week of seventy years, Messiah was cut off, but the nationality of Judah was not at that time overthrown. The Christ came between law and gospel, or Benjamin and Judah, as the feet of Judah, yet the nation of Judah was not overthrown till the destruction of Jerusalem by Titus. The scepter left at the coming of the law of gospel, but the nation was not at that time overthrown.

The laws which God will have to make David, or the kingdom, are the civil law as given in the seventh head as judges, of whom Joshua was first, and the seventh head as gospel, or the apostles, of whom Andrew was first.

These are Levi and Judah, or Benjamin and Judah. In this land they are the seventh judge as Levi, or Andrew Jackson, born of Levi, and Bishop Andrew, the head of the seventh church, born of Judah.

The feet of Judah, as gospel, given to Japheth, are Napoleon Bonaparte and Cromwell of England. Each of these are the seventh to make the feet of Judah, as in Japheth, or Rome. The scepter left Judah in the one foot by the Roundheads under Cromwell, and by the tragedy of the Jacobins under Robespeire and company, which brought forth Bonaparte that took the scepter in the other wing of Judah as his feet in the coming of the law given to Judah, in the land of Japheth's enlargement. The tribes to represent these seven heads twice counted in the land of Japheth, to set the gospel given to Judah are the Puritan or Plymouth, of the extreme North, and the Orleans territory of the extreme South. Between these extremes as the feet of Judah, or gospel, given to Japheth in Europe, the nation of Benjamin and Judah, was set up. The law-giver had been, according to a regular line of descent, until the coming of these two seventh heads in Europe, to show that the scepter had departed from Judah. If Cromwell seized the scepter in England, Bonaparte found it, in his own language, in a gutter upon the cont'nent of Europe, and he took it. This scepter of law, whether for civil or soul, did not leave Judah as gospel in Rome, and in England, till the rise of the two men aforementioned. Nor did it leave this Judah till the coming of the lawgiver, as the United States, between these tragical endings. Nor did this nation arise as the law-giver, but between the extreme representatives of these tragical endings of Judah in Rome, as the extreme North and South.

As between these political extremes as "the feet of Judah for the Israel of law, so the feet for the gospel of Judah, stood as Episcopal Ruth and Presbyterian Orpha. Elizabeth and Cromwell, make these feet of Judah, from between which the church of John Wesley arose. If he was not the promised "Shiloh" as the head of the church, or the first apostle, Andrew, he is the forerunner to bring Andrew. If he said "slavery was a great evil," it is Andrew who by divine appointment, will teach what Paul taught upon the subject, "Let servants count their own masters worthy of all honor that the name of God be not blasphemed." Teach this as a truth, Timothy, till God in his seven times, to demonstrate truth, shows who is the only and "blessed potentate and king," by the establishing his own laws for both soul and body as given by Christ and Moses.

The tribe of Benjamin in this land moves not more exact with the law of the land, than does the tribe of Judah in national Judah fill his prophetic part. Between these two tribes Jerusalem is built. "If Leah left bearing" at Judah, or Georgia, as the last of the first settlement, Rachel died at Benjamin, or Texas, as the last of the second settlement of the Israel of both law and gospel.

Let us read the prophecy of Jacob concerning Judah as the law-giver according to the fulfilled facts:

The tribe of Judah, the law-giver, shall never have a

civil head in Israel until Shiloh, as the head of gospel, or the church, comes of him. The scepter will then depart from national Judah, and the first civil law-giver, the tribe of Judah will have, will be the one from "between his literal feet" as his literal twins, made up of the two territories he gave the nation. Bishop Andrew, who was born of the tribe of Judah, came as the head of gospel, in the year 1844–6. The scepter left national Judah in the year 1847, upon the passage of the "Wilmot Proviso," by the lower House of Congress; then it was that the law of equal rights in Israel departed from Israel, and the eagle of America, like that of Pagan Rome, became the law-maker for Judah. That that was Israel, and who claimed to hold the covenants, persecuted the Shiloh that came of Judah and said, "Away with him, away with him." God will give us a king, according to our understanding of what his word teaches, as interpreted by the laws of nature and not the written laws of God. God says, his law-givers are out of Judah; man says, they are out of Benjamin; God says, the laws of Judah are the king of Israel; man says, they are out of Benjamin; God says, what I have written shall remain; man says, change the name of reproach, and write it, he said he was king of the Jews; God says, change it not, it is the Methodist Episcopal Church, *South*; leave that reproach there, Pilate, I will make it good. This is the bride to David, whether as Washington, the first judge, or Jackson, the seventh, or Polk, as the last of the seven, or as Davis from "between the feet of Judah" at the second annointing of David by national Judah, as the first law-giver, that Judah gives the nation. As gospel Judah was in sack-cloth for forty-two months in the land of Japheth, or Europe, or 1260 years, so shall these laws as husband and bride, in national Judah, be as dead for forty-two months, or 1260 days, upon a union of the two with Ham as a servant, as "the head stone of the corner." These as civil and soul laws, are the world's Elias as the God servant to save it.

When this Judah binds Japheth as his own foal to the vine, or civil law, he takes "Issachar as the ass, or servant," and binds him to Joseph as the church, or "choice vine," because he is the representative of Ham that followed the laws of nature, or the beast, yet he has a soul to save, and God demands this of Japheth, or Judah. His church's garments he washed in wine, as the grace of God, while his clothes he washed in literal blood, like "the master, who trod the wine-press all alone." These laws of God have built that Jerusalem that was to be "inhabited as towns without walls for the multitude of men and cattle therein." They, as the representatives of the laws of God are that Jerusalem of which it is said, "though all nations burden themselves with Jerusalem, they shall be cut in pieces." This Judah is a lion's whelp, and as the representative of the laws of God, he has been driven about in the world ; " he stooped and he crouched," when once he is upon his feet, " who then will rouse him up.

God will have his forms of laws united as in Tubal-Cain and his sister Naamah, or as in Simeon and Levi, yet not by statutory law. The demonstration of the truth will supercede the necessity of any statute law upon the subject. The church, like the daughter of Jeptha, will be devoted to perpetual virginity, or like Abishag to David of whom it is said "David knew her not." The two will never be allied by civil law, yet by universal consent at the third and last annointing of David in the year 1944–5, or after another cycle of Orion, or at the end of fourteen more generations, or presidents, in this land, giving to each six years. David will be annointed as Solomon by universal consent. These laws, whose heads come of the tribe Judah, in national Judah, are " the stone out of the mountain," or they are " the ancient of days," because they stand for the laws at first set up by God himself. With these laws the saints " shall take the kingdom ;" " the stone out of the mountain shall fill the world." This stone was first Levi or S. Carolina, then the seven that move as the '' seven eyes of God," that put up the civil law in Naphtali. All the world will come to these in a civil sense. It was said of the church at Philadelphia " The world shall come and worship at thy feet, and they shall know that I have loved thee." It is said of Judah, " Thy father's children shall bow down to thee." "Judah shall have his hand in the neck of his enemies ;" " from the prey thou art gone up, my son."

This Judah stands for both the civil law as " States rights, " local charters," that was first put up in this Israel at Philadelphia, while the church of John Wesley, that was first set up at the same place, represents God's laws of the soul, " Ye must be born again."

The law of the church, as at first set up, did not conform to the law of Moses in a civil sense, and hence it required a second settlement of Israel to make national Judah show what is both law and gospel.

Let these thoughts suffice for Judah, while we pass to consider the double character of Joseph.

Joseph is the type of the double laws, which bring the heads of the laws of Judah. At the birth of Joseph, Rachel said. " The Lord hath harkened to my petition, and taken away my reproach." Jacob, in blessing Joseph, gave him such a blessing as is not written in anything in the book or out of it. It is too long to write, but sums up all things, "From heaven above and the earth beneath, and to the uttermost bounds of the everlasting hills: blessings on the head of him who was separate from his brethren." Joseph, moving as the laws of God for which he stands, has been reproached in all the world. As God has determined these laws shall take the world, the farthest verge of the universe will be brought under their dominion. These laws are Moses and Elijah, that have power to smite the earth. Of Joseph it is said, "From hence is the stone the Shepherd of Israel." As a stone they break; as a shepherd they gather. When the brethren of Joseph sold him, Reuben plead for him, and had him placed in the pit, intending to take him away. When the church represented by Joseph divided in this land. it was a son of Reuben. the Rev. John Early, (now Bishop,) that tried to get the church to pass over the division for four years. It was to no use—the time had come for Joseph to be taken away. When the civil head divided, it was that same Reuben that called the convention at whose head sat one of her distinguished sons (John Tyler) to see if Reuben could not take him away. The types must be fulfilled, and all of Reuben's efforts were in vain. Joseph was "two years in prison. He was seventeen years old when he was taken captive, and he was thirty years old when he stood before Pharoah." The church was in prison from 1844 to 1846. From 1844 to 1861-3, when it was taken captive, are seventeen years, and it will be thirty years before it will have a presidential head, or in 1874-6, that will hold its doctrines as taught by Moses. In other words, Abraham, as law, will be circumcised when he is ninety and nine years old, or in 1875, at which time Ishmael, the son of the bond-woman, that came up with Mr. Lincoln's proclamation of 1863, will be thirteen years old, and he too will be circumcised, or, what is the same thing, conform to the law of the flesh as given in God's Book. The law of the flesh stands to the Japhetic Israel as the law written in the flesh before the law was finished. The writer has written these thoughts more extensively in a larger work not expedient to be given the public at this time, and we cannot dwell in this outline.

In reference to the law-giver as the civil head, "They put his feet in fetters," as David said they did to Joseph. He too was in prison for two years, and he is God's agent to show which way the law moves. Like the master, he was taken from prison and judgment, and whether he will, like David, outride the storm and come off conqueror, or whether he will be crucified by the mob, time will show. One thing is positive: he came from the tribe of Asher, of whom it is said, "As thy day is thy strength shall be." So long as he is of use in God's demonstration, "so long will he be used." In reference to who belongs to Joseph as the church, it is said of him, "blessings of the breasts and of womb." This is given to show that Joseph as the church has little ones connected with it. There is no need for further debate upon either Greek prepositions or verbs upon this subject. Circumcision was the outward sign down which to look for the "Shiloh" upon whom the laws of God were to meet in the Israel of Shem. When this law in the flesh, and by which an oath was confirmed, by placing the hand on the flesh, was supplanted by the written law of the flesh, baptism became the outward sign down which line the world was to look for the nation to bring forth the laws of the kingdom. It was not through Confucus, nor Zoriaster, nor Mahomet, it was to come. According to the literal types, it was to be through Naamah, and Ruth, and John the forerunner, and Andrew. Not only was the church of Japheth to come through this line, but the head of the civil was to come through the same line. The church was to bring the civil, according to the promise made, that the "seed of the woman down the lines of Cain and Seth, should conquer the seed of the Serpent or Nahash." The line from Cain and Seth, as civil and soul that met in Lamech, in Philadelphia, was the place of union of the two; as to place which union made that Joseph that was first sent away to his country and people from England as the "earth that helped the woman."

It was in Naphtali, after the same two had been as Joseph sent away the second time, that "Rachel prevailed." These, as civil and church laws, were each organized upon the same laws. The head of the church, like the judiciary of the civil, was for life. If the law of the one was elective for four years, so with the other. If the civil located its head as a place in Catholic Maryland, the other went to the same place to get its first bishop, in 1774. If the one has its lower and higher courts, with the right of appeal, so has the other. If the one went into Manassah to get its heads of division, so did the other go into the same tribe to complete its division. If the one, as law or Abraham, went through the land from the Atlantic to the Pacific ocean, so did the other.

We remember, some years ago to have read a speech of the Hon. Henry Winter Davis, made at an Episcopal Convention in some northern city. When the question of sending the gospel to California was before the convention, the honorable gentleman stated, that while they were debating the question, the Methodist church had taken possession of the land. How well this agrees with the blessing on Joseph. "Joseph is a fruitful vine, whose branches run over the wall." The Methodist Episcopal Church, South, is God's chosen bride for the husband by such an array of testimony it seems no way is left by which man can dispute it. God is after the law of both the body and the soul, as these were given by Moses and Christ. Nothing less than these for the double man will answer the purpose God intended. Since the world began, these never met in an organized form, according to God's laws, as Joseph, till they met in the civil government of this South land, as put up in Naphtali and the Methodist Episcopal Church, South, who as the church stood to represent Naphtali as a character, when, as a "hind let loose, he gave goodly words" by publishing his law, in conformity to Moses, upon the service of Ham as a servant of tribute." This question is so easily understood it is hardly worth while to show its truth. The Israel of Shem, or the Jews, had a ceremonial law for the soul. The Israel of Japheth had a king for the civil and also the ceremonial for the soul. The Israel of this land of Japheth's enlargement had the civil law, but there were seven churches to represent the soul. One of these seven only dates from the tribe of Judah as the lawgiver. This was the one that was put up at Philadelphia after forty years journeying in the wilderness. This was the one of the seven that was promised to be kept, and at whose feet the world was to worship. This was the one that divided in 1844, and it was the Southern wing of this one, that conformed the church law to the civil law as given by Moses in the character of Naphtali in 1860–1. Then it was that Joseph, or Rachel, as the book of God, " prevailed."

As God's demonstration leaves nothing to the conjecture of men, either as to civil or soul laws, the contest in this and land of Israel, as to forms of laws, is not between Naomi Ruth, as Rome and England; nor is it between the Episcopal Ruth, as the church of England, and Presbyterian Orpah, standing for all the Congregational churches, but it is between the two wings of the church of John Wesley, that date from Philadelphia. Let us examine into these, and see what God teaches as between them.

It has been a question of disagreement between the parties composing the church of Mr. Wesley, whether the church, in its official head, holds an order as Bishop, that is higher than that of a Presbyter. The church in England follows the order of the Presbyter, while in the United States he appointed it a bishop. As an office, he was appointed to be the general superintendent; as an order by his ordination, he was a bishop. In the published debates of the division of the church in 1844-5, the northern wing took the ground that the superintendent was an office and not an order. The southern wing took the ground, that as an order it held for life, from which the individual could not be disposed except for malfeasance.

God purposely involved the difficulty, to show his plan was that the church had a head—that to "Paul was committed the care of all the churches." How was this question settled in the division of that church, which dates its rise in this land from Philadelphia, yet dates its head with a bishop from Catholic Maryland?

In order to arrive at the answer to this question, we must go back to the types, as set in the Israel of Shem. The tabernacle of Moses, the first and second temple by Solomon and Zerubabel, were literal symbols of the church, which was set up by Christ and the apostles, of whom Andrew was the first. Who built the literal tabernacle with Moses? A man of Judah, and a man of the tribe of Dan. Who built the first temple? Accounts are doubled in reference to this question. This is intentional. One account says, "it was a widow's son of the tribe of Naphtali." The second says, "it was a widow's son of the daughters of Dan." The second temple was built by Zerubabel and Joshua, "the high priest." To whom in this land do these characters refer? They have respect to the bishops that stood at the head of the southern wing of the church in this land at its division. Who are these? Bishops Joshua Soule and James Andrew. From whence came they in this land? The one is from the tribe of Dan and the other is from the tribe of Judah. Joshua Soule came from Dan of the North, and came into Dan of the South. The State of Tennessee is the tribe of Dan in the South, while Georgia is Judah. Are these the men to build the tabernacle with Moses? The very same. From which tribes did they come? The tribe of Huram sent the man of Dan out of the North. Dan in the South as Tennessee, was a part of the tribe of Simeon or North Carolina, in the South, as the second son of Jacob, so the tribe of Simeon, the second son of Jacob, in the first settlement, was Plymouth, or Massachusetts, and his tribe of Dan that came of him was Maine. If from this tribe of Dan in the North, Joshua came, he came into Dan of the South.

As moves the soul, or church, so moves the body, or civil law of the body. If the vice-head of Mr. Lincoln, as Hamlin, came of Dan, or Maine, in the North, so his second vice-head as Andrew Johnson, came of Dan in the South. Let this pass, as we are following God's demonstration of the law of the church.

Joshua Soule was born of Dan, or Maine, in the North, and came into Dan, or Tennessee, of the South. He was the son of a widow women, whether of Naphtali, or Dan, for the reason that in neither case did the church have a husband. It was not established by law to make it a husband, nor did it conform to Moses as the husband. The church was in the hand of Naphtali, or the Levites, but this Naphtali, though traveling as "a hind," it was not a "hind let loose," because she was governed in two respects by the laws of men and not the laws of God. God selected two heads to correct two errors and with which to build the tabernacle.

In the trial upon Bishop Andrew about slave-holding, "No fault was found against him." Yet in order to reach him, the office of a bishop was lowered and held to be only an office and not an order. This placed filthy garments upon "Joshua the high priest," who was the chosen agent of God to work with Zerubabel in building the gospel temple. God's prophet commanded those that stood by to take the "Filthy garments off of Joshua the high priest," and clothe him with change of raiment, and set a fair miter upon his head, all of which was done by the church, South, when it held to the three orders in the ministry of bishop, priest and deacon.

In the names of Joshua and Andrew, the civil and gospel compound together as body and soul. The seventh head of law as judges, had for its first judge Joshua. The seventh for gospel was the apostles, of whom Andrew was first. In compounding these in this land, as the heads of the church, they are Joshua and Andrew. As between these two sevenths, surnames were given to men, so Joshua holds the given, and Andrew the surname. The symbolic names of these are Joshua Soule, as body and soul. That of James Andrew is "law and gospel." One other name stands symbolically for the same—it is "Judah Benjamin," Jefferson Davis' Secretary of State. That fact that holds with the church, as gospel, is the same with the civil heads, or judges of this Japhetic Israel. The first judge, as George Washington, is the synopsis of all the judges in Israel. Thomas Jefferson is the doubting Thomas that divides the apostles, the same as the second half of this Israel beyond the Jordan divides this Israel. That second half was bought by Thomas Jefferson, and it is given to show to this Israel it is the doubting Thomas in reference to the laws of God. James Madison is James the greater, and is the father of the laws of this Israel. "James the less," is James Monroe, and with him the nationality of the Israel of both law and gospel was cut off. With him, as law, the first Israel as unity ended, and the second demonstratively began by the adoption of the Missouri Compromise. Andrew Jackson, is the apostle of law, and is given to show unity in Israel, though demonstratively it is duality. John Tyler is the apostle John that brings the first and the last, by bringing Benjamin as law, which tribe is Texas. His name is John as the Revelations. As the literal John brought the Benjamin as "the lone star," standing for the law of Moses, so will the millennial John bring the law of Moses for the world. James K. Polk, as law, closed the line, as with him law went through the land. Let the reader attempt to apply these truths to the seven northern judges of this Israel. This may be done to the two that Simeon of the North had, as the two Adams', in the days of Israel's unity, and then again to the last as James Buchanan, that closed the line with James, while all the rest will be as much confused as Babylon. These are Martin, and William, and Millard, and Franklin. Any accident in this arrangement? No accident in anything. Israel has never made one mistake, according to the types. Anybody to be praised or blamed? No! no! no! Nothing but the God of the world showing he is king, and he is going to rule by his own laws.

Cyrus delivered the literal tribes from the literal Babylon. God said of Cyrus, "I have surnamed thee," hence the surnames of the representatives of the laws of God in this Japhetic Israel.

The gospel that Christ gave became in Rome "the man of sin," that united civil and soul laws in the Pope of Rome. The gospel of this land that dates from Judah, has in the North, as the Methodist church, become "the man of sin" by a union of civil and soul laws, according to the laws of the natural man. The Southern wing of that church stands as the "doubting Thomas" in reference to God's own laws concerning Ham as a servant of tribute. These will never doubt again after this tragedy ends, nor will it ever again be said, "Cotton is king." God's witnesses are his written laws that have been in reproach long enough. These are the world's tormentors. They are constantly crying, "Down with your natural king; down with your natural religion." The man-child, as Joseph, has been shot at, and men may rejoice at their death. It is only for a measured time this rejoicing will be had. They will stand upon their feet again. "There is none like unto the God of Jeshuron, who rideth upon the heavens in their help." The eternal God is their refuge and underneath them are the everlasting arms, and he shall thrust out the enemy from before them, and shall say destroy them.

While there are a multitude of individual characters, that are used as types in the Israel of Shem, and are given to find their anti-type in the Israel of Japheth, such as Ahithophe, Hushi, &c, yet as these are not required in this synopsis, we let them pass.

It was said by the law-giver "that the twelve apostles should set on twelve thrones, judging the twelve tribes of Israel." It was in the trial of Bishop Andrew that this was fulfilled. As it was Catholic Rome that betrayed the Savior in that they departed from the law of gospel, so in this Japhetic Israel, the resolutions to depose Bishop Andrew came from Catholic Maryland.

This was the tribe chosen to act the part of Judas among the twelve apostles. Christ said, "Mine own familiar friend, in whom I trusted, lifted his heel against me." Maryland was a slave-holding State and should have stood with her sisters in the trial of the beloved bishop. God's demonstration required it otherwise. The two other tribes, or States, or apostles that journeyed with the others in the South, and upon whom "lots were to be cast to fill the place of Judas, were Delaware and Texas. Bishop Andrew was tried in 1844 and in 1845, the nation cast the lot, and Texas as Mathias, took the place of Judah. A double act by this is represented, showing that the same method of "casting lots for an apostle," likewise applies in a civil sense. That principle first adopted by the first bishop, as Francis Asbury, is this law of God. Asbury was appointed to the office by Mr. Wesley, yet he refused to be ordained to the office until he was elected by "casting lots for him." God is always in the lot whether in making a tribe or a bishop. That Judas, which betrayed Bishop Andrew for thirty pieces of silver, has repented and thrown down the money, saying, "I have betrayed innocent blood," by returning to his brethren This fact, like almost every other, was written by the writer before it came to pass. This Judas has another part to act; he holds the nations bag, and in him the nations law-makers meet. The honorable councellor has failed. Let that pass.

Let us dispose of this tribe, Judas, in this connection. "Rahab, the harlot," in literal Israel, is the same as Tamar, the harlot, in gospel Israel. It was at the union of church and State by Constantine, that Tubalcain, and his sister,

Naamah, turned Tamar, the church of gospel, to a harlot. This Naamah is the same as Naomi, the mother-in-law of Ruth and Orpah. The dividing line between Naomi and Ruth, was drawn between the two daughters of Henry VIII, as Mary and Elizabeth. Catholic Mary is Naomi, Protestant Elizabeth, is Ruth. The tribes in this Japhetic Israel to represent these are Catholic Maryland and Virginia. It was Rahab that saved the twelve spies, represented by the two as Joshua and Caleb. It was Naomi, or Mary, that saved the twelve represented by the two as Old and New Testaments in Rome. It is from, or in, Catholic Maryland, in this Israel, the two take their rise in this land. While the civil as law, holds its seat in Catholic Maryland, it was in her the church as gospel took its head, or first bishop, in 1774. It was promised Rahab that she should be preserved amid the overthrow of the idolatrous Canaanites. That unity of laws, which met in her God, means to preserve upon the principles of his own government, and not as they have been corrupted by men. The same is true in reference to the unity that exists between civil and soul laws in Ruth. When she says to Naomi, "Where thou diest I will die," it is to be understood that as unity upon human principles, both Ruth and Naamah will end, yet as a type of God's unity neither will die.

Let us now come to the most interesting part of this, the grandest demonstration of truth the world has ever known.

It has been told before, but it is so ingeniously concealed that even the thoughtful reader may not have discovered it. It was shown in the beginning that the two cherubims were Moses and twelve patriarchs, and Christ with twelve apostles. The one was written in four books of law, and the other by four evangelists, and that the ark was veiled in the middle by four great prophets and twelve minor ones. It was likewise shown that the characters and symbols of the Old Testament were transferred to those of the New Testament, and that these held the relation to each other of body and soul.

Has the reader discovered that those tribes in this land, which came of the four original mothers, have become substitutes of the mothers in their symbolic character? And not only this, but that the three tribes that were bought on the west of the Jordan are the substitutes of the whole of law, gospel and the prophets, and of all that has been taught by the first half of Israel?

The two sons of Rachel are Benjamin and Joseph, but Benjamin is law, and Joseph both law and gospel, Who stands to represent these in this Israel? Benjamin is Texas, and Joseph is Ephraim. or Missouri, that is to become "Multitudes of nations." Who is Gad? He is the dividing tribe of Israel, and stands for all the prophets. Is Gad " the seer of David," the same Gad as the literal tribe of Gad represented by Arkansas in this land? The very same. Who is David? He is civil law and soul law—that is, he is Moses and Christ, or Benjamin and Joseph, with all the prophets as his seer. With these prophets the ark is veiled. Are these three tribes that make the ark bought tribes? Every one of them has been bought with thirty pieces of silver. Has it been the price of blood? With oceans of blood, from Abel down to this " tree of knowledge " it has been bought. The lower story of the ark is Benjamin, or Texas, as the law of Moses. The upper story is Ephraim, or Missouri, or Christ. The middle story, as the prophets, is Gad, or Arkansas.

Have these transfers come all the way from Noah, or from God's covenants with Abraham, to arrive at this truth? Let us see how this has been done. The first covenant given to Shem as law was the "first.born son," and ended at the coming of Christ as the "first begotten son," and the covenant was changed from the body, or law of the body. to the soul, or law of the soul. This second covenant was for gospel, and was given to Japheth in Europe. While Benjamin is law, yet the Israel of law, with its ceremonial law, became Reuben, the first born son of Jacob, after it divided. The gospel given to Japheth was Joseph, yet when that divided, it became Simeon and Levi, in Rome. The first and second wings of Israel became Reuben as the first in Shem, and Simeon as the second in Japheth—that is, the law that Levi as Moses gave became Reuben, and the gospel that Judah gave became Simeon and Levi, as civil and ceremonial.

Who stands to represent these in this restored Japhetic Israel? The first and second sons. The first as Reuben is Virginia; the second as Simeon is Plymouth. These are the first and second as halves in the first settlement of Israel as law. If the head of this Reuben was Elizabeth, the head of Simeon was Cromwell. The tribes which these gave the nation are representative tribes of those characters which these heads have acted in Israel. As Israel become dual'ty in Shem, so have the tribes of Reuben holding the northwest, become duality in this Israel. As it was through Ruth, or Elizabeth, the churches head has come, so the civil head, as the half tribe of Joseph as Manassah, or Kentucky, or as the son of Reuben, he is Bohan, to set the northern boundary of national Judah, come through Elizabeth, or

Reuben, or Virginia. If this one tribe that came of Reuben stands for the two tribes as Benjamin and Judah in the division of the Israel of Shem, the other five of Reuben, as Ohio, Illinois, &c., will stand for the ten as Ephraim under Jeroboam. This son of Reuben, as Kentucky, becomes the substitute of Reuben; As Simeon and Levi were joined as one, so the tribe of Dan in the North, is the representative of that forcible unity; this tribe is Maine, the son of Simeon, or force in the North. In the first settlement of this Israel, the phrase from "Dan to Sheba," means from "Maine to Georgia." In the second settlement the phrase from "Dan to Sheba," means from "Tennessee to Texas." This forcible Simeon of the North will become as Ephraim, the younger of the two half tribes of Joseph; then will the prophecy of Jacob be fulfilled in reference to the two sons of Joseph, "These shall be mine—as Reuben and Simeon they shall be mine." These two as half tribes shall become the substitutes of law given to Shem, and gospel given to Joseph. They shall become the substitutes of "unstable Reuben" in this land and of "cruel Simeon." That which stood for Simeon and Levi in Rome as forcible union to one church, or which stood as Simeon of the North, or Plymouth, upon the original doctrine of Levi, of "freedom in religion," since Leah took the husband in 1821, has become forcible in Levi, the same as Simeon was in Rome. The Church must think as the State dictates. This is by God's appointment, "Cain shall bear rule over his brother." "The body shall rule soul." The civil shall rule the church till the time appointed. This forcible Simeon of the first settlement, as the second son, is transferred to Simeon or North Carolina, as the second in the settlement of the Israel of both law and gospel. The tribe which came of this Simeon is Rachel's, and becomes the substitute of forcible Simeon. This tribe is Dan or Tennessee. He teaches "the voice of the people in their tribe capacity, is the voice of God, when according to the law Moses."

The two laws which come of Judah, stand for both soul and body, and are Levi and Judah. The two tribes of Judah are the substitutes of these laws—these are Asher and Naphtali, or Mississippi and Alabama. These are unity in Naphtali, and are the same as Joseph, as his two sons, Manassah and Ephraim. The substitutes of the two bought tribes are those laws as civil and church, which stand as their opposites, forty years from their coming.

These are the very same as the two of Joseph, or the two of Judah, and these are civil law and soul law. In every case they are the civil government of the seven tribes that first set up the Southern Confederacy and the church government of the Methodist Episcopal Church, South. It is the most complicated, yet the most exact, demonstration of truth, that this world ever saw. It is the summary of all prophecy and of all history.

This is God's method to overcome the confusion of Babylon. Men need no longer to learn Hebrew and Greek to find the truth. God has moved out a long ways from this confusion. Let such as would learn come to God's teaching. You have his book, you have his history, you have it all acted over again in this grand summary. Come here and learn. You need not be afraid you will exhaust the subject. You may gaze, and wonder and adore, until, like the writer, you will feel that you ought to cover yourself with sackcloth and ashes, in view of your littleness, and ignorance and corruption. Reader, would you study these truths enough to learn the great lesson they teach, and then read the books and papers that are teeming from the press, and the laws of all the law-makers, you would feel, as did Elijah, that the wicked had taken possession of God's inheritance, and that you were the only one left in all the land. You would feel that you would prefer to be hidden with God in the lonely cavern, or in the humble dwelling of the poor widow, than to be lifted to the highest honor Ahab or Jezebel could confer.

Will the world come to these demonstrated laws of God? They are the "man-child that the woman, or Bible, has brought forth that is to rule all nations with a rod of iron. The plagues of the book will be added to men till they cease to mend it. These are the same laws that were first set up at Philadelphia for both the civil and church, and they hold "the key of David."

The world shall come and worship at the feet of this Joseph as the laws of God. The archers have been shooting at them, and a thousand gallows have been made upon which to hang them, yet they will take the world. How will this be done? In the same manner that the four States or tribes, as Reuben, Simeon, Dan and Gad, come to the seven that first put up the civil government in Naphtali. For whom does Reuben stand? He stands for the Israel of law, or the Jews, and also for Ruth as the Episcopal Church. Will these come? These will come according to the type set by Reuben in this summary of God's Israel.

Will Simeon as Rome, or Simeon as the Congregational or Presbyterian churches come? All of these will come. These will come as did the tribe of Simeon down to the seven that stand as the "seven eyes of God." Will all in all lands come who hold that every nation should be the judge of its own laws? All these will come, as did Dan, by the consent of its inhabitants. Will all who hold the doctrine of equilibrium, or balance in power, come? All of these will come as did Gad come to the seven that first set up this government. These are given as God's synopsis to show how the world will come. God's laws will subjugate the world, "beginning at Jerusalem." The stone out of the mountain in the land of Japheth, is the nation to take the kingdom. The greatness of the kingdon shall be given to these because "the hair of his head (or the laws to govern him) are like the pure wool." "The waters will be first to the ankles, then to the knees, then to the loins, and until they become an impassible river. As the tribe of Manassah began the second journey in Israel, so the first great battle of Manassas was the synopsis of this seven years contest. Time will show in what respects we have erred.

It now remains to measure the prophetic times that set the history of Israel's movements. That this question may not be clouded with an excess of explanations in assigning the reasons to set the points from which to date the measures, facts are all that need be stated. While the prophet Daniel is the leading prophet, given to measure the times of the Japhetic or gospel Israel, the symbol for the predicate of the prophecy belongs to the Israel of Shem. Daniel speaks of Israel as one, without respect to the three different theaters of Israel's action, as in Shem or Asia, Japheth or Europe, and America as the land in which "Japheth is enlarged over Shem" The apostle John, who uses the same measures of Daniel, (in some respect,) shows that Daniel had respect to gospel Israel as to measure, but to the Israel of Shem as the literal act upon which the symbol for the measure is based.

As everything in the history of Israel has its corresponing opposite in the type, so it must find its corresponding opposite in the anti-type. Let this point be illustrated by an example or two taken in this land, in reference to annointing David, as both civil and soul laws. In the first settlement of this Israel, the literal acts of Oglethorpe and the Rev. John Wesley, in the tribe of Judah, find their corresponding opposite in both civil and church laws forty years to Philadelphia. The same is true in reference to the coming of the two tribes of Issachar and Zebulon. Each of the acts by which these tribes came into Israel finds its corresponding opposite in the second annointing of the laws of David, forty years from each. Let these examples answer upon this point. As David was annointed three times to be king in Israel because of the laws of God which met on him, the same as in the literal ark of Noah, three times must the "man of sin," as the corresponding opposite of David, or Joseph, be set up for king, while the laws of God, or the woman was in the wilderness. These three annointings of the "man of sin," stand as the "abomination of desolation," to the laws of God. As Daniel uses three measures of time for the three fold ending of this "man of sin," each of these measures must be applied to the different periods that mark the "abomination," or man of sin, on account of human laws, instead of the laws of God, in order to reach the whole sense in the fulfillment. The literal abomination in the Israel of Shem, was the forcing of literal Israel to eat swines' flesh, or the placing of heathen idols in the temple of Jerusalem. The meaning of this was the forcing any human laws contrary to the laws of God. Any law of man contrary to God's written law after the completion of the law is "the abomination of desolation."

The Christ is the Abel, whose blood had to speak from the ground for forty and two months from "the abomination of desolation." The laws of "the Christ" are the Christ. The two sons of God as "the first born" and the "first begotten, met on "the Christ. These are God's laws given by Moses as "the first born" and by Christ as the first begotten." Whatever has been exalted to power by human laws during the forty-two months or 1260 years, these were to "speak from the ground, or prophecy in sackcloth," is of man, and cannot be the laws of God.

The three points from which to date the measures of Daniel are first, the Union of church and State, under Constantine, in the year 325 A. D. In this union the church was subordinate to the State and existed by the will of the State. The second annointing of "the man of sin" in the gospel to Japheth was in the time of Justenian, when he as Emperor of Rome, claimed the property of the citizen, as the property of the church, and confiscated it for the churches benefit. If Constantine laid the foundation for the civil division of Rome by building the city of Constantinople, Justenian prepared the way for the churches division by the building of the church of St. Sophia, at Constantinople, which he said excelled the temple of Solomon.

The point from which to date this elevation or annointing of David, upon human laws, was in the years 530–3 A. D. That which was subordinate to the civil with Constantine, was regarded its equal in the code of Justenian, and the church became a joint heir with the State as to the rights of property.

The third and last act of this "abomination" was when all the tribes in gospel Japheth, said all power in both departments of the kingdom was given into the hands of the Pope of Rome, and in whom the church or soul swallowed up the body, contrary to the teachings of God, that the "blood of Abel," was to speak from the ground for "forty and two months." From the best light before us, nine of the ten kingdoms of West Rome in the land of Japheth acknowledged the supremacy of the Pope in both civil and soul laws in the year 606. These nine stood for one foot of gospel Judah, given to Japheth, while England as the other foot did not acknowledge the Pope's supremacy tell the year 608 A. D.

These stand for the three annointings of David as civil and soul laws in Rome, or Japheth, and set the times from which to date the three different measures of times as used by the prophet Daniel, when they are used as a day for a year. These three measures are 1260, or 1290, or 1335 years. The last measure is a blessing on those who come to the 1335 years.

As there are three points from which to date these measures, each of the three endings at 1335 years, will be with some great good to the people with whom they end. At the last of which, David, as the representative of the laws, or son of God, will be crowned " Lord of the world."

Let us now take the points that are well defined as the "abomination that takes away the daily sacrifice," because the civil head interferes with the prayer to God as " the daily sacrifice," and see how they have ended in the fulfillment. If to 325 be added 1260, it is equal to 1585. This is about the middle of the reign of Queen Elizabeth, when that which became forcible union with Constantine was liberated by toleration under England's first protestant queen.

The twenty years service of Jacob to Laban began his exodus back to his "father's laws." If to 1585 we add the twenty years for Jacob to gather up his family, it will end in 1605. It was in the following year that Sir W. Raleigh began the settlement of the tribe of Reuben as the exodus of the Japhetic Israel. If to 325 we add 1290, it is equal to 1615. It was the year following that the citizen began to claim civil rights by a clear title to the domain upon which he lived in Reuben, and not in the name of the crown. If to 325 we add 1335, it will be 1660, and is the year in which Charles II was restored to the throne of England, whose father had been beheaded by the Roundheads under Cromwell. This was the blessing at the end of the 1335 years to the original land of Japheth. Let these same numbers be applied to the second annointing of the abomination in the year 530–3.

If the first as 1260 be added to 533, it is equal to 1793, and is the year in which the Jacobins beheaded Louis of France, which stands as the other foot of gospel Judah given to Japheth. If to 531 1290 be added, it is 1821, and and sets the time in this Israel of Japheth, when the Israel of both law and gospel was to be cut off by the Missouri Compromise line.

That which began the exodus with Elizabeth and Reuben, in one foot of gospel Judah, measures from the other foot the Israel of both law and gospel. The same facts that apply to the individual tribes of Israel in this land, apply also in the measures of the tribes from the land of Japheth, or Europe. If to 533, the last number as 1335 be added it will be 1868. At which time the king in this land may be restored as in England. This will be upon the law of God as given by Moses and Christ, and not upon human laws.

Applying these several numbers to "the man of sin," yet the type of the laws of God, the same as Joseph, or David, in the person of the Pope of Rome at 606–8. They will stand thus, 606–8 added to 1260 equals, 1866–8, this is the time for the standing up of the two witnesses of God. The one as the church and the other as the civil. If Melchezedek as the church stood upon his feet in the year 1866, the civil as Abraham ought to be upon his feet by the close of 1868. No convocation of the church since the first Christian Emperor, Constantine, was ever more important or freighted with greater results than that which met in the South land of Jacob at New Orleans in 1866. It was God moving by his own types and measures of his own prophetic times.

We pretend not to dictate in any matter but only follow where God leads the way. If the writer wrote before it came to pass that that church would not remove that name of reproach, (South) it was because the types pointed that way. This sect is God's chosen Rome to claim the world. Rome was a name of place; *South* is a name of place. But then it is a reproach. God said it should be reproached till his appointed time. The first name as Methodist was given in "reproach," when that became popular in this land, God's measured times were not up, hence another name of "reproach" was required, this was found in the word "South," which was synonymous with "pro-slavery." Both were reproached as Moses and Christ; these had to be reproached. Does God despise the day of small things?" Who art thou, O, great mountain; before the God of the world, thou shalt become a plain." God's reproached witnesses shall become the head of the corner. "The God that answers by fire will be God." Let men call Abra-Ham an old fogy. Let them say of Noah he was drunk, and there is no need to regard the madness of a drunken man. Let men dictate to the God of the world, and burn up the bible unless it teaches as they say it ought; while from the depths of the soul that is within us we pity them; we are impotent to arrest the storm, and can only bid them drive on ; you will find out whether there is a God that rules in the affairs of men, and that rules by his own laws before it is done. Man has been a fool ever since Adam and Eve begat the "Nahash ;" he can learn in but one school. Like the child, he must get burnt before he knows what is the meaning of the word fire. No use for God to tell him it will burn him ; he must feel it before he will believe it. Man is the same thick-headed dolt, at this day, that he was in Adam. "Let that tree alone," had about as much influence over Eve as God's laws, "Thou shalt not covet thy neighbors servant," or as "Servants be obedient to your masters," have over the world to-day. In answer to these laws of God, it is nature, that is, it is the beast that says otherwise.

If the church has a bishop, he is not to be diocesian; he is to be a bishop in all places and at all times, ready to perform the office of a bishop. He can be no more restricted in the office of his calling than can that of a son of Aaron, who is called to go into all the world and preach the gospel. An office may be confined to place; not so with an order.

It is the order of God that none but the Levites shall take down the ark and set it up. Whatever others may do in reference to temporalities, they are forbidden to buy their priests, as did Micah, and hence the necessity of a head to the church. It does not appear that this can be allowed when the church reaches the point set by Jacob, as "God the Holy Ghost," of giving a "tenth of all to Levi." This is the standard set by God, and when Jacob reaches the laws of God for which he stands, expressed by his father's house, it does not even then appear that the church will be allowed to buy her priests. Let these thoughts pass, as we are measuring prophetic times.

The 1260 from the time " the little horn," or " man of sin," came up among the ten horns, or kingdoms of West Rome, ends in 1866–8 This ending of the 1260 years from the elevation of the Pope in 1868, is the same time as the 1335 years from Justenian, of which time it is said, "blessed is he that waiteth and cometh to such time." This time brought back the literal king to Judah in " the earth that helped the woman," and it would indicate that mighty events by this double ending are to take place in national Judah. As it is no great ways in the future, let us not speculate.

If the second number as 1290 be added to 606–8, it is equal to 1896–8. By which time not only the "beasts of this land will be slain, but all the other beasts that hold dominion on this continent will have that dominion taken away."

If to the 606–8 the last number of 1335 be added, it will be equal to 1941–3. At which time the laws of God will be crowned king, as was David, by all the tribes; not only by the two tribes of Benjamin and Judah in this land, but by the ten tribes of Japheth, or Europe. A range of five years from 1940 to 1945, will include the ending of all prophetic measures of time; God's truths will then become so plain, time need be no longer counted according to the prophets. From that date will begin the thousand years rest of Israel from wars and strifes, and military schools will be done away with.

Let us look at these a little. This seven years war will separate Rachel from Leah by showing the world for what laws these stand. Rachel is the word of God for both body and soul. Leah mixes up the laws of God with human laws. The seven years war of the Revolution in this land got both Leah and Rachel to Jacob, which lasted for one cycle of Orion, or eighty-four years, in which there were fourteen generations or heads of political government. This ended, and Israel went into captivity. There are fourteen generations from the captivity to Christ. This fourteen will include another cycle of Orion, or eighty-four years. These will not be great heads of civil government as in West Rome, or England, each of which had seven from the gospel as Abraham to the rise of David, as "local charters," "States rights," nor will it be heads as presidents in this land with seven from the North, and seven from the South, but it will count by time, and six years will make a generation, because six times fourteen are eighty-four. If to 1860 eighty-four be added, it will be 1944; so if from 325, as the time of union under Constantine, 180 years be added as the Sabbatic day time of 1260 and 180, as the Sabbatic years in the 1260, these will sum up as follows, 325 added to 1260, 180, 180 equals 1945. Again, Noah was building his ark 120 years. The time this ark began to be built in this land, was when Israel separated in the year 1821. If 120 be added to 1821, it is equal to 1941. Again, Job lived after his second lot of children were settled one hundred and forty years. This second lot of children began at the purchase of the second half of this continent in the year 1803–4. If to this 140 be added, it is equal to 1943–4. Thus it will be seen that all the measures of time agree with the fourteen generations yet lacking from the captivity to the crowning of Christ, as the second Adam "Lord of all."

In the siege of Jerusalem, Ezekiel was commanded to lie 390 years upon one side and forty years upon the other. (A day is a year.) The three hundred and ninety days begins about the time Luther set aside the law of Rome concerning marriage and took a wife, and extends down to about 1944–5. The forty years has been twice fulfilled in this Israel. Once from Judah to Philadelphia for the first settlement of Israel, and once from Ephraim to Naphtali for the second settlement. Perhaps it may be replied that this year 1944–5 does not complete the world's last chilaed of a thousand years. If it did, the teachings of Christ, concerning the shortening of the last days, for the elect's sake, would not be understood. Had not God cut short the last chilead, his own laws would have been driven out of the world. As it is, most persons think they are gone and will never return again. These will learn better at the time appointed. God's witnesses are only dead for a little while. As the church is upon her feet, so the civil as given by Moses will rise again. Israel is murmuring about this Moses that has brought here into this wilderness. Let Israel hush complaining. Things may look a little frightful with the sea in front, and the mountains on either side, and an army in the rear, and the "pillow of fire and cloud" lighting up Israel's enemies. No marvel, that under these circumstances the Ham-an should think himself the one chosen to be honored by the king, and that it is his "manifest destiny" to exterminate Israel. The little queen has made her petition to the king in a week of prayer by all her people, and a day of fasting. God speaks to Israel, "stand still." "An east wind" will divide the sea, at "The time appointed," "A Cyrus will be found to dry up the Euphrates. A Samson will tie the foxes tails with a fire brand between them." Could a voice as humble as the writer's be heard in Israel, we would say, "stop your complaining." None but Noah, Daniel and Job will be left when God sends the sword in the land. Say your prayers and trust the God that sees and hears and knows all things.

It would be a pleasure to the writer to accompany the reader through that seemingly mysterious prophecy of Ezekiel, contained in his 38th and 39th chapters. This is a specific prophecy of a great civil war, in the latter days of the restored Japhetic Israel. We are prevented from this by these running outlines, which have already gone beyond their prescribed limits. From what has been said in the synopsis the intelligent reader can learn to read it for himself. It will well repay the effort.

We have now tracked God's symbolic characters from Adam and Eve, Cain and Seth, Shem and Japheth, down to the tribes in this south land. The double prophecy of Noah is the foundation for the double covenants with Abram and Abra-Ham. The seed of the literal Jacob, as twelve tribes, are the types of the spiritual Jacob as twelve tribes, and also as the twelve apostles. The question is before the reader, and is more worthy of his study than any other question the world has.

Let us drop a word to the sons of Levi, or more properly the sons of Aaron. "Called of God, as was Aaron." Preach God's word as he has given it. Do not mend it. It is the power of God to the salvation of the world. If thou lift up thy tool upon it, thou hast polluted it. If it says, "There was a man of the land of Uz, whose name was Job," preach it that way. God will take care of results, If it says "there was a father that had two sons," preach it just that way. "Lift up thy voice like a trumpet, cry aloud, spare not." Tell every hairy Esau he must become not only smooth Jacob in body, but he must become "wrestling Israel in soul." Tell him he must "tremble exceedingly" to do this according to the type set by Isaac. If you daub with untempered mortar, for fear the refined or that the elite will leave you, you are not serving "the master," but are looking for your reward in this life. This was not the way your type, the servant of Abraham, who stands as "God the Father," acted when he was sent to bring a bride for Isaac. Never did man urge the claim of his master with more forcible arguments or with greater earnestness. Nothing for himself; everything for his master. Take pattern, my brethren. Take pattern: here is your model, given by God himself, of how you should plead for the master.

Perhaps you may think an obscure, unlearned farmer has no right to address you thus. Pardon one of the humblest ones in God's creation. The light is so clear. The question is one of such eternal moment, that while we hold no orders, we are constrained to speak a little, and mean no offence. Would you, as a reviewer, feel inclined to take us to task? Let the writer talk a little, and then he will thank you for doing so. It will do no good to use that very convenient argument, "He hath a devil," or he is deranged. Such an argument as this is strong evidence that, in the absence of all others, this is the last resort. You need not ask,

"Have any of the scribes of Pharisees believed on him?" We answer, No; they have not been asked to believe. How can they believe before they have heard what the babbler would say? You need not complain of our grammar, or of a want of elegance in turning periods. We have endeavored to use the best language to convey thoughts at our command, and have hardly looked into a grammar for thirty years. You need not quote human authorities, except upon a matter of history. In using human opinions as your standard, you contradict the declarations of the Book of God, that "no man, in heaven nor in earth, could unseal the Book." God himself had to do this with a nation. This nation is "the lion of Judah" among the nations of Japheth. Every tribe in this Judah is a talking prophet, and God has selected it himself as the "world's law-giver. Upon his shoulders the world's government will rest." This Judah is the "wonderful counsellor," to teach the divine will. Would you review and instruct the writer? You must take God's types, and God's prophets, and God's history as he fufills them, and come down to the work like a man in search of truth. If you will do this, and point out our defects, you will then find the writer one of the most ready learners and willing disciples in all the land. Unless you can do this, you need not attempt it by any other means. Big thoughts, all round about, is what the writer loves. Tinsel and display will do very well in their place. When thoughts are small, there ought to be some substitute. Every blunderbuss known to the armory of war cannot batter down Gibraltar when charged with mustard seed. We are indifferent whether the reviewer's thoughts came (as the writer's) jostling along upon a dray, or whether, if the writer choose, they are roun-tired and flounced from head to heel, sparkling with diamonds and pearls, riding upon the dashing locomotive. It will make but little difference, if the thoughts be there, whether they fly as on eagles wings, or creep on all-fours. If you should attempt a review, and calculate that by high-sounding words, or by bringing up the antiquated opinions of those who never lived to see this day and time—those who never looked upon national Judah—it will be to no use. It may be that the humble writer is as well informed upon these points as his would-be reviewer. No lopping and pruning will answer the end. The writer admits, in advance, a multitude of minor defects, about which he is, perhaps, too indifferent. You must dig up and exterminate, in order to overthrow. "Moses and the prophets" are our only guides. While the means used in their fulfillment are not regarded as extraordinary, yet God has never left himself without a witness. The results accomplished are more striking than any miracles addressed to the natural senses. These are a talking miracle. They will speak to the world, and not alone to the immediate beholder.

Let us glance at the manner in which God, by ordinary means, works miracles in the gospel dispensation given to Japheth. Moses and Christ had denounced Jerusalem. Who shall bear witness to the truths these have uttered? Is it a christian? No; he is a biased witness. Is it a Roman? He knows nothing of the denunciation and the laws of Israel. Who shall it be? It is both the commanding general and the high priest of the literal Israel. Providentially was he preserved, that he might be an eye witness to bear testimony in all things to the teachings of Christ and Moses. The preservation of Josephus, may not be regarded in the light of a miracle, yet none can read how it was done but will conclude there was something wonderful in it.

When the time came for the seventh head of Pagan Rome to arise, it was Christian Constantine. Who can sit in judgment upon Constantine in reference to that cross in the heavens, and the voice he heard, "By this conquer."

The prophet John said this seventh head should come, and thus it came. The same prophet had said it would "continue a short space." Thus it was as Julian, the nephew of Constantine, apostatized from the Christian faith of his uncle. Again, Christ had said Jerusalem should not be rebuilt. The apostate Julian said it should. He was the Emperor of all Rome, who can hinder? Two tribes of Israel had once rebuilt the temple with opposers from every quarter. None now stand to oppose the Roman Emperor. Did he rebuild it? He did not. Why? Balls of fire bursting from the earth drove off his workmen. Any miracle in this? Nothing but the collected gas in the old rubbish, and the cavities of the former building. Any miracle about it? Nothing but Moses and the prophets. Look again. When the time came for the day to break, by bringing the "woman" out of her hidden place, two young men are walking the field and a flash of lightning kills one of them and sends the other to be a monk. In his lonely cell he finds the "woman." The world's light chained to a block. The world's only hope hidden in a dark place. Was that flash of lightning that sent Martin Luther into the convent a miracle? It was "Moses and the prophets." If Moses told how "the day would break," the prophets tell when it would be done. Look again. While Luther brings the woman from her hidden place to instruct the world, the Spanish Jesuit is preparing the whip of cords to drive Israel in another quarter. If the teachings of that "woman," organized the gospel church in this land at Philadelphia on the 4th of July, 1773, it was the same year in which the Pope of Rome abolished the order of the Jesuits. "The beginning of one is the end of another." Look again, when the time came to cleanse the sanctuary at the end of 2300 years, John Wesley is the chosen agent of God to do it. He was the son of an humble curate, out of a lot of eight children; when his father's house was on fire, he alone was in the upper story. Appearances indicate he must perish. Will he perish in the flames? The eye of God is there. God has a special use for him and he shows the world, "I go where no man's building is." He will not be burnt up. Any miracle in it? No miracle, but Moses and the prophets. If Moses said one must rise and go into "Red Esau's" land and return to "wrestle with the angel," Daniel says, "The sanctuary of the heart shall be cleansed." If Wesley filled the literal act of Jacob, moving as "God the Holy Ghost," in the other case he taught the doctrine of the Holy Ghost, "Sanctification is through the spirit and belief, in the word of God."

As Rome, by her confessional, had broke up the service of the literal Ham as a servant of tribute, as God brings back the gospel of Christ, so he brings back the law of Moses. In drawing the line between Catholic Mary and Protestant Elizabeth, Elizabeth comes back to Moses. "Canaan shall serve Japheth," and is a negro-trader. No miracle. Nothing but Moses and the prophets. "In chains shall Ethiopia come over to thee, and they shall be thine"— Isaiah. When God draws the line of the church of gospel in this land, while the one wing held only one bishop, who was a non-slaveholder, as Bishop Andrew, God removed his beloved wife, and made him marry a slave-holding woman. Is this a miracle? It is Moses and the prophets. "Not by power, nor by might, but by my spirit." God intends no disputers shall contend with him. Moses had said, Reuben should bring Benjamin. In order to its fulfillment, God had to remove Gen. Harrison. Moses had said, the scepter should leave National Judah when the head of the church came of the tribe of Judah. In order to its fulfillment, God removed Gen. Taylor. Are these acts, with hundreds of others, miracles? They are Moses and the prophets. "I will settle you after your old estates, and restore your presidents as at the first." Look, reader, look around you; an overwhelming array of testimony meets your gaze, look which way you will. No need for one to come from the dead, and teach differently from Moses and the prophets.

Were this possible, he could only be regarded as an evil spirit from Pluto's dark dominions, wandering to and fro in the earth to create evil among men. Will men believe it? Not till the time appointed. God will keep the veil over their faces till he finishes what he has undertaken. God has determined that "Days shall speak and the multitudes of years teach wisdom." These must turn the page as they move along for man's enlightenment.

In this same sense was this great civil war in this land foreseen and laid down from the beginning. It was Lamech with a double work to do in slaying an "old man as the divine right of kings," and a "young man" as the divine equality of Ham with Shem and Japheth.

It is vain for men to talk of peace, when there is no peace. There can be no peace only between the christians. Moses is one, Christ is the other. The civil man is Moses, the soul man is Christ. These are "the sons of God." This is the demonstrated truth of God in this land. It is an act of sovereignty alone upon the part of God to select the four hundred thousand slave-holders in this land to teach the world law and gospel. While the normal relation of Ham is that of a "servant of tribute,' Ham has a soul. Ham is unlike either Shem or Japheth, in that he has no religion. His religion is just that the superior brothers give him. He is ready to be circumcised with Shem, or take the gospel with Japheth, The supple cast of his nature throws the burden of his religion on Shem and Japheth. God will hold these to account about how they act towards Ham. He is an idiot in understanding the laws of God, yet he is in the image of God. In order that Shem and Japheth may bring him to the laws of God, it was necessary that they should control the physical man. Hence he is a "servant of servants." In any other relation, he is a beast, and God can not hold Shem and Japheth responsible for him.

Abra-Ham is the "possessor of heaven and earth," and "Heir of the world." This is the decree of God. The Hamman, or natural man, standing opposed to Abraham, contests every inch of the ground against God and his laws. The conflict is long and desperate, yet the issue is foretold. Egypt, Babylon, Ham-an, all tell how it will end. God will show his word alone is "The tree of life." "Do to others as ye would they should do to you," with men, beasts, birds, all in their normal place, is the law of God. Man cannot change the ass to a horse, nor an ox to an ass. In the atonement of Christ, all are one. In the law of Moses, these are parent and child, husband and wife, master and servant, king and subject.

As to whether the negro of this land was in truth the literal descendant of Ham, has no more to do with the question, than whether in very dead Abraham is "God the Father, and Isaac is God the Son, and Jacob is God the Holy Ghost." Each of these are the symbols of the things for which they stand. The literal man for which the symbolic Ham stood had to come from Africa in the "last days," as the land of the assignment of the lot of Ham. From there he comes, and the negro, taken in a literal sense, is the man that would never cover a naked world with the laws of God for its government.

Ham is the literal type of all men who follow the laws of nature, and not the laws of God. As Ham is governed by his physical senses, so these are governed by physical laws. In either case that which is mostly prized is that which can be used by the physical man. Ham is in every sense of the word a cash workman. He must see a present benefit from a present action. He is always like Ham-an, early in the court for fear some other claim will come up before his. He has no trust or confidence beyond what he sees and feels.

And now, my countrymen, North, South, East and West, the author of this humble work is nothing but an humble follower of the calling of Cain. He has never been set in any manner to enlighten the world upon anything. He was hardly out of sight of his humble home since he has had a being. He has not written to bring himself into notice. These thoughts may fall still-born upon the public mind till the time appointed. That God has a use for them, is a truth. God does not work for nought. If he brings forth a nation to tell the world his laws, that nation will do it at the appointed time. If the laws of nature could have "unsealed the book," it would have been done long ago. They have been traced from Adam by God's own symbols down to the tribes of this south land. The thoughts of the writer are more concerned about the duties of the undertaken and the great hereafter, than about any notoriety he can receive from his fellow-men, either as being a disputer or as being wise. We love all men in all lands, whether they belong to Shem, Ham or Japheth. We are ready to help every one with that ability that God hath given us. We love our country, and have been taught to revere its laws.

We have submitted to confiscations and thefts, and to more than these. We have not complained. We can submit to any indignity in the way of further hardships and confiscations—these we can endure. We can submit to yield the life we hold, if God so require it, much as we desire life; much as we love our fellow-men, and country, and wife and children, and even life, we love the word of God more than these. We cannot willfully and knowingly take a "solemn oath" and take it falsely, which "God abhors," to help you say, that Ham is equal to Shem and Japheth. Excuse us, my countrymen, and we would plead for thousands of others in this land who follow the written laws of God. These would do the same thing if they lived in "Scandinavia or Australia." We do not believe that the God that made the world is jesting with his fellow creatures. He said Canaan should serve Shem and Japheth; that he should be a "servant of servants." We cannot bow to the Ham-man that says otherwise than this. We allow you to be as honest as we are, and believe you feel that you are doing "God service." We think you feel thus because you follow the laws of the "Nahash," or natural man or Ham-man. You honestly think the same concerning us. God will, in his own time and in his own way, settle the difference between us. In conclusion, we subscribe ourselves, what in truth we are, "not one" but the "voice of one."

A VOICE.

www.ingramcontent.com/pod-product-compliance
Lightning Source LLC
Chambersburg PA
CBHW030350170426
43202CB00010B/1327